IMPACT
SOCIAL STUDIES

Our Communities

INQUIRY JOURNAL

Mc
Graw
Hill

Program Authors

James Banks, Ph.D.
University of Washington
Seattle, Washington

Kevin P. Colleary, Ed.D.
Fordham University
New York, New York

William Deverell, Ph.D.
University of Southern California
Los Angeles, California

Daniel Lewis, Ph.D.
The Huntington Library
Los Angeles, California

Elizabeth Logan Ph.D., J.D.
USC Institute on California and the West
Los Angeles, California

Walter C. Parker, Ph.D.
University of Washington
Seattle, Washington

Emily M. Schell, Ed.D.
San Diego State University
San Diego, California

mheducation.com/prek-12

Send all inquiries to:
McGraw-Hill Education
120 S. Riverside Plaza, Suite 1200
Chicago, IL 60606

ISBN: 978-0-07-691376-3
MHID: 0-07-691376-7

Printed in the United States of America.

12 LMN 24 23

E

Program Consultants

Tahira DuPree Chase, Ed.D.
Greenburgh Central School District
Hartsdale, New York

Jana Echevarria, Ph.D.
California State University
Long Beach, California

Douglas Fisher, Ph.D.
San Diego State University
San Diego, California

Nafees Khan, Ph.D.
Clemson University
Clemson, South Carolina

Jay McTighe
McTighe & Associates Consulting
Columbia, Maryland

Carlos Ulloa, Ed.D.
Escondido Union School District
Escondido, California

Rebecca Valbuena, M.Ed.
Glendora Unified School District
Glendora, California

Program Reviewers

Gary Clayton, Ph.D.
Northern Kentucky University
Highland Heights, Kentucky

Lorri Glover, Ph.D.
Saint Louis University
St. Louis, Missouri

Thomas Herman, Ph.D.
San Diego State University
San Diego, California

Clifford Trafzer, Ph.D.
University of California
Riverside, California

Letter from the Authors

Dear Social Studies Detective,

Who were the first people who lived in your community—and why did they choose to live there? In this book, you will find out more about communities. You will think about the issues important in your community and what **you** can do to help!

As you read, be an investigator. What do you wonder about? Write your own questions and read closely to find the answers. What in this book interests you? What do you find exciting? Take notes about it and analyze your notes. Then you can use your notes to do a project to share what you've learned. Take a closer look at photos of real people and places. Use maps and time lines to think about how your community has changed.

Enjoy your investigation into the amazing world of social studies—a place where people live in communities that grow and change, a place where **you** can make a difference!

Sincerely,

The IMPACT Social Studies Authors

San Francisco Bay Bridge in the 1940s

Contents

Reference Sources

Communities in Our Country and World

 Why Does It Matter Where We Live?

Chapter 2

The Community and Its Environment

 EQ What Is Our Relationship With Our Environment?

Chapter 3

People and Communities

 What Makes a Community Unique?

Chapter 4

Communities Change Over Time

 How Does the Past Impact the Present?

American Citizens, Symbols, and Government

Why Do Governments and Citizens Need Each Other?

Chapter 6

Economics of Communities

How Do People in a Community Meet Their Wants and Needs?

Skills and Features

Inquiry and Analysis Skills

Reader's Theater

My Notes

Getting Started

You have two social studies books that you will use together to explore and analyze important Social Studies issues.

The Inquiry Journal

The Inquiry Journal is your reporter's notebook where you will ask questions, analyze sources, and record information.

The Research Companion

The Research Companion is where you'll read nonfiction and literature selections, examine primary source materials, and look for answers to your questions.

Every Chapter

Chapter opener pages help you see the big picture. Each chapter begins with an **Essential Question**. This **EQ** guides research and inquiry.

In the **Research Companion**, you'll explore the EQ through words and photographs.

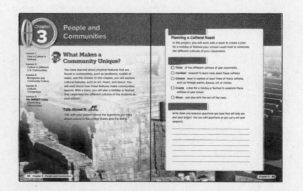

In the **Inquiry Journal**, you'll talk about the EQ and find out about the EQ Inquiry Project for the chapter.

Explore Words

Find out what you know about the chapter's academic vocabulary.

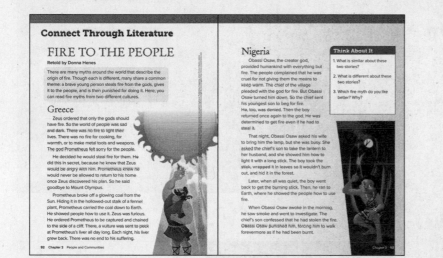

Connect Through Literature

Explore the chapter topic through fiction, informational text, and poetry.

People You Should Know

Learn about the lives of people who have made an impact in history.

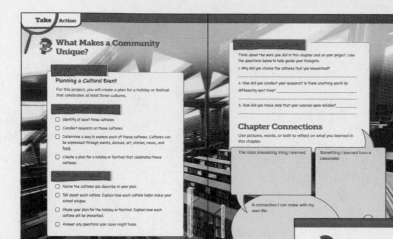

Connections in Action

Think about the people, places, and events you read about in the chapter. Talk with a partner about how this affects your understanding of the EQ.

Take Action

Present your Inquiry Project to your class and assess your work with the project rubric. Then take time to reflect on your work.

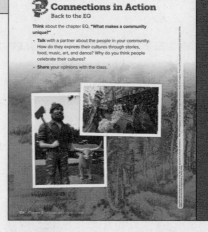

The IMPACT Today

Take what you have learned in the chapter and tie it to your community. Consider how key questions related to geography, the environment, culture, history, government, and economics impact us today.

Every Lesson

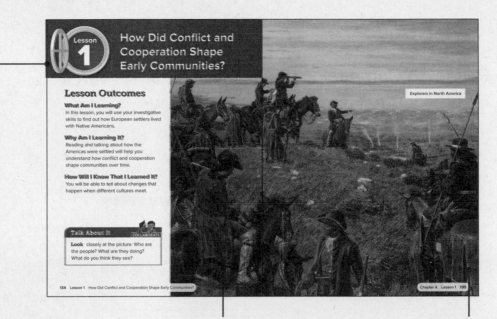

Lesson Question
lets you think about how
the lesson connects to the
chapter EQ.

Lesson Outcomes help
you think about what you
will be learning and how it
applies to the EQ.

Images and text provide
opportunities to explore
the lesson topic.

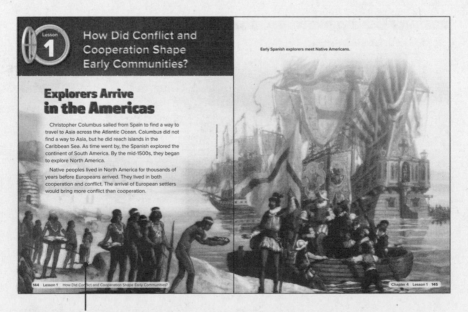

Lesson selections help you develop a deeper
understanding of the lesson topic and the EQ.

Analyze and Inquire

The Inquiry Journal provides the tools you need to analyze a source. You'll use those tools to investigate the texts in the Research Companion and use the graphic organizer in the Inquiry Journal to organize your findings.

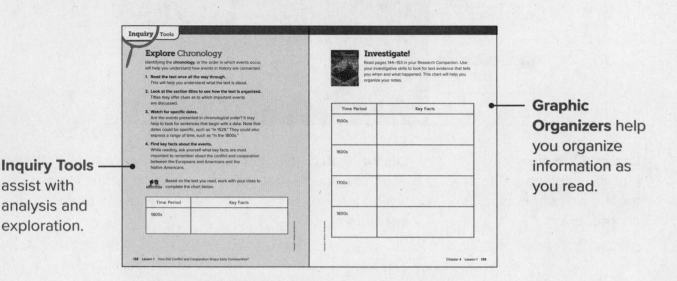

Inquiry Tools assist with analysis and exploration.

Graphic Organizers help you organize information as you read.

Primary Sources let you read the words and study the artifacts of people from the past and present.

Maps show where events happened.

Stop and Check boxes provide opportunities to check your understanding, consider different perspectives and make connections.

Report Your Findings

At the end of each lesson, you have an opportunity in the Inquiry Journal to report your findings and connect back to the EQ. In the Research Companion, you'll think about the lesson focus question.

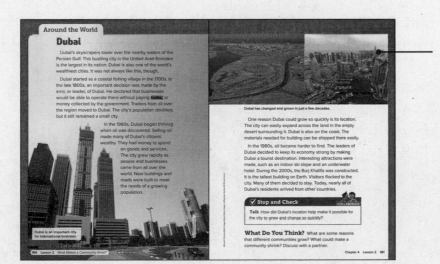

Think about what you have learned.

Write about it using text evidence to support your ideas.

Connect to the **EQ**.

Think about what you read in the lesson. How does this give you a new understanding about the lesson focus question?

Why Does It Matter Where We Live?

In this chapter, you will explore communities in the United States and around the world. You will read about the features that make these communities special. You also will learn about the ways these features affect how people live, work, and play. With a team, you will create a travel brochure about your community.

Talk About It COLLABORATE

Talk with your partner about the questions you have about communities in the United States and the world.

Understanding Your Community

In this project, you will work with a team to identify features in your community. Then your team will use pictures, words, and maps to create a travel brochure about your community.

Project Checklist

- ☐ **Think** of how your community is different from other communities.
- ☐ **Choose** at least three features that make your community special.
- ☐ **Conduct** research to learn more about these features.
- ☐ **Determine** how to present these features in a travel brochure. What might a photograph, a written summary, or a map tell about each feature?
- ☐ **Create** a travel brochure that uses pictures, words, and maps to tell about your community.
- ☐ **Share** your travel brochure with the rest of the class.

My Research Plan

Write down any research questions you have that will help you plan your project. You can add questions as you carry out your research.

_____

_____

_____

Complete this chapter's Word Rater. Write notes as you learn more about each word.

climate

- ☐ Know It!
- ☐ Heard It!
- ☐ Don't Know It!

My Notes

_____

_____

_____

community

- ☐ Know It!
- ☐ Heard It!
- ☐ Don't Know It!

My Notes

_____

_____

_____

elevation

- ☐ Know It!
- ☐ Heard It!
- ☐ Don't Know It!

My Notes

_____

_____

_____

erosion

- ☐ Know It!
- ☐ Heard It!
- ☐ Don't Know It!

My Notes

_____

_____

_____

humidity

- ☐ Know It!
- ☐ Heard It!
- ☐ Don't Know It!

My Notes

_____

_____

_____

landform

My Notes

☐ Know It!

☐ Heard It!

☐ Don't Know It!

_____

_____

_____

natural resource

My Notes

☐ Know It!

☐ Heard It!

☐ Don't Know It!

_____

_____

_____

population

My Notes

☐ Know It!

☐ Heard It!

☐ Don't Know It!

_____

_____

_____

precipitation

My Notes

☐ Know It!

☐ Heard It!

☐ Don't Know It!

_____

_____

_____

region

My Notes

☐ Know It!

☐ Heard It!

☐ Don't Know It!

_____

_____

_____

Where Is My Community and What Is It Like?

Lesson Outcomes

What Am I Learning?

In this lesson, you will use your investigative skills to explore different kinds of communities and where they are found.

Why Am I Learning It?

Reading and talking about different kinds of communities will help you understand more about your own community.

How Will I Know That I Learned It?

You will be able to write a paragraph about your community and why people choose to live there.

Talk About It

COLLABORATE

Look closely at the pictures. Which place is more like your community? Explain your answer.

Copyright © McGraw-Hill Education

A rural community

An urban community

1 Inspect

Read the text and look at the map and the photos. What do maps and photos show?

Circle words you do not know.

Underline clues to help you answer these questions:

- What is a map?
- What is a satellite image?
- What community is shown in the satellite image and the map?

My Notes

_____

_____

_____

_____

_____

_____

Maps and Satellite Images

A map is a helpful tool. It is a drawing that can show where streets, parks, and other landmarks are located in a community. A map is different from a photo. A photo shows an image of the actual community.

A satellite image is a photo of a place taken from high above it. In a satellite image, you can see the roofs of buildings, treetops, cars, and sometimes even people. If there are a lot of trees, some streets might be hard to see.

A map does not include every detail. A map shows only the things that make it a useful tool. For example, a street map shows clearly where streets are located. People use street maps to see how they can get from one place to another in their community.

A satellite image can also be a helpful tool. It shows what a place actually looks like from above. You can see where buildings are located and the type of land a place has.

A satellite image of Detroit

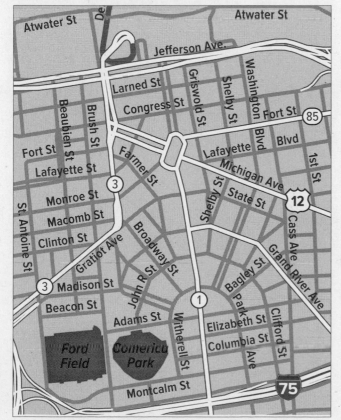

A street map of Detroit

2 Find Evidence

Look Again How can you tell that the same community is shown both in the satellite image and on the map?

Circle a location in the photo. Then circle the same location on the map.

3 Make Connections

Talk Think about the communities shown in the photos on page 7. What might you use a street map of those communities for? What might you use satellite images for?

COLLABORATE

Explore Summarizing

When you **summarize**, you find the most important ideas you read or see. Then you tell these ideas in your own words. Summarizing can help you remember information.

1. **Read the text all the way through.**
   This will help you understand what the text is about.

2. **Look for the most important details.**
   Details tell more about the main idea.

3. **Explain the text in a sentence or two.**
   When you summarize, you use your own words to tell the most important ideas from a text.

 Based on the text you read, work with your class to complete the chart below.

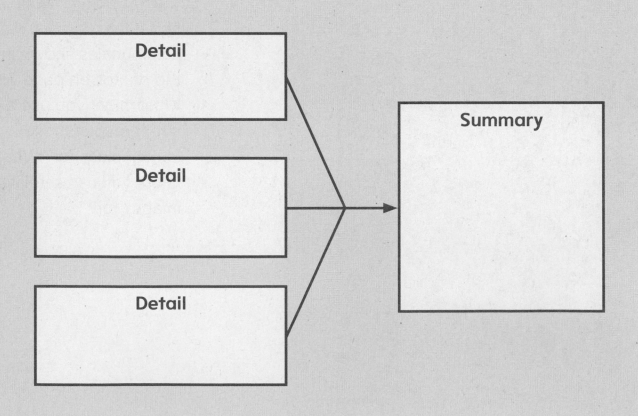

Investigate!

Read pages 8–17 in your Research Companion. Use your investigative skills to look for text evidence that helps you summarize what you have learned about locating and describing communities. This chart will help you organize your notes.

Detail

Detail

Detail

Detail

Detail

Summary

Think About It

Give an Opinion

Based on your research, what kind of community do you live in: urban, suburban, or rural? Why do you think people choose to live in your community?

Write About It

Write and Cite Evidence

Based on your research, write a paragraph that identifies the type of community where you live. Why do you think people choose to live there? Use facts from your research to explain your answer.

_____

_____

_____

_____

_____

_____

_____

_____

_____

_____

Talk About It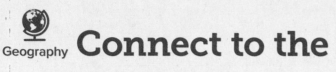

Share Your Ideas

Share your paragraph with a partner. Discuss features of your type of community.

Geography

Connect to the

Pull It Together

How do the features of where you live affect life in your community?

_____

_____

_____

_____

_____

_____

Inquiry Project Notes

_____

_____

_____

_____

How Does My Community Fit In With My Country?

Lesson Outcomes

What Am I Learning?

In this lesson, you will use your investigative skills to explore the regions of the United States.

Why Am I Learning It?

Reading and talking about how the regions are alike and different will help you better understand what makes each region unique.

How Will I Know That I Learned It?

You will be able to write a paragraph identifying the region where your community is located and explaining what makes it an interesting place to live.

Southeast

Talk About It

COLLABORATE

Look closely at the pictures. What do you notice? What things are the same in these pictures? What things are different?

Northeast

Midwest

Southwest

West

The United States can be divided into five main regions: Northeast, Southeast, Midwest, Southwest, and West.

1 Inspect

Read the title. What do you think this text will be about?

- **Circle** words you do not know.
- **Underline** clues that help you answer the following questions:
  - Why do many people go to visit the Gateway Arch?
  - Why was the arch built?
  - What does the arch look like?

My Notes

_____

_____

_____

_____

_____

_____

_____

_____

Going West!

The Gateway Arch is located in St. Louis, Missouri. The arch is named for the role St. Louis played as the Gateway to the West in the 1800s. Many people who traveled to the West started their journey in this midwestern city.

The arch reaches 630 feet across and stands 630 feet tall. That is twice the height of the Statue of Liberty. It is made of 5,199 tons of steel. That is over one million pounds. The arch can sway up to eighteen inches in high winds.

The Gateway Arch is part of the Jefferson National Expansion Memorial. This place honors President Thomas Jefferson's plan to make the country larger. He wanted Americans to settle the land to the west. The arch also honors the people who set out from St. Louis to reach the West. Underneath the arch, a museum tells visitors the story of Westward Expansion. Six areas feature interactive exhibits that celebrate the spirit of those who made the journey west.

The Gateway Arch was completed in 1965.

The Museum of Westward Expansion is underneath the Gateway Arch.

Visitors can ride in a special train through a tube to the top of the arch. The arch has sixteen windows that face east and sixteen windows that face west. People can look out on the city and the surrounding land.

Monuments help us to understand the role history plays in everyday life. An arch is a type of doorway. Think about the choice to make a monument to the journey westward by building such a structure. Why do you think this is important?

2 Find Evidence

Look at the pictures.
Reread the text. What do you learn about the Gateway Arch that you do not learn from the pictures?

Underline the details that describe the way the arch is built.

3 Make Connections

Talk Turn back to page 15. Find COLLABORATE the pictures that show the Midwest and the West. What does the Gateway Arch help you understand about how these regions are connected?

Explore Main Idea and Details

The topic is what a piece of writing is about. The **main idea** is the most important point the author makes about a topic. **Details** tell about the main idea.

1. **Read the text once all the way through.**
   This will help you understand what the text is about.

2. **See if there is a sentence that states the main idea.**
   This is often the first sentence of a paragraph. Sometimes other sentences in a paragraph can state the main idea.

3. **Now look for details.**
   Sentences with details give more information about the main idea.

 Based on the text you read, work with your class to complete the chart below.

Topic	Main Idea	Details
Gateway Arch		

Investigate!

Read pages 18–29 in your Research Companion. Use your investigative skills to look for text evidence that tells you the main idea and details about each of the five main regions in the United States. This chart will help you organize your notes.

Region	Main Idea	Details
Northeast		
Southeast		
Midwest		
Southwest		
West		

Think About It

Review your research. Based on the information you have gathered, in what region do you live? What features describe your region?

Write About It

Define

What is a region?

_____

_____

_____

_____

_____

Write and Cite Evidence

Write an opinion paragraph explaining what makes your region an interesting place to live. Support your opinion with reasons.

_____

_____

_____

_____

_____

Talk About It

Consider Opinions

Find a partner who chose a different reason than you did for why your region is a good place to live. Take turns discussing your opinions and the evidence used to support them. Do you agree or disagree with your partner's opinion? Why?

Geography

Connect to the

Take Action

What are some characteristics of your region? Why do these characteristics matter to your community? List ideas to share with others.

_____

_____

_____

_____

_____

_____

Inquiry Project Notes

_____

_____

_____

_____

Lesson Outcomes

What Am I Learning?

In this lesson, you will use your investigative skills to learn about climates in the United States.

Why Am I Learning It?

Reading and talking about different climates will help you understand how climate affects the people, plants, and animals around you.

How Will I Know That I Learned It?

You will be able to write a diary entry that explains how climate affects your community.

Talk About It
COLLABORATE

Look closely at the picture. What do you think is happening? How could this impact the community in the picture?

Copyright © McGraw-Hill Education

In some climate regions of the United States, snowstorms like this are common.

1 Inspect

Read Look at the titles of the two graphs. Based on the titles, what do you expect to see in the graphs?

Circle the month with the highest average low temperature in International Falls, Minnesota.

Discuss with a partner how the weather described in the graphs compares to the weather in your region.

My Notes

_____

_____

_____

_____

_____

_____

Climate Helps Describe a Region

The climate of a region makes a big difference! Climate is the weather a region has over a long period of time. California's Death Valley is the hottest and driest place in the United States. There is very little **precipitation**. In an average year, there may be less than two inches of rain. This can be very challenging.

Living in a cold climate can also be challenging. Keeping homes, offices, and schools warm in a cold climate can be expensive. Blizzards can cause power outages.

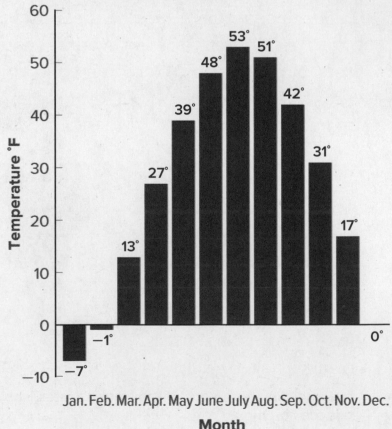

Average Monthly Low Temperature in International Falls, MN

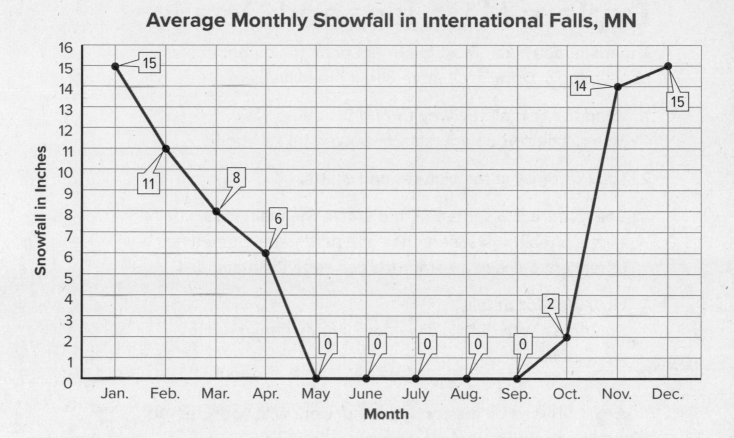

Average Monthly Snowfall in International Falls, MN

Snowfall in Inches (y-axis, 0–16)
Month (x-axis)

- Jan. 15
- Feb. 11
- Mar. 8
- Apr. 6
- May 0
- June 0
- July 0
- Aug. 0
- Sep. 0
- Oct. 2
- Nov. 14
- Dec. 15

One of the coldest communities in the continental United States Is International Falls, Minnesota. In an average year, International Falls gets almost six feet of snow and over two feet of rain. This amount of precipitation is challenging, too. Snow can make it difficult to get to school and to stores. Rain can cause flooding.

2 Find Evidence

Look How does the information in the graphs help you understand the climate of International Falls?

Reread According to the text, how are Death Valley and International Falls similar?

3 Make Connections

Talk Look at the photo on page 23. With a partner, discuss the climate shown in the photo. How is it similar to the climate of International Falls, Minnesota?

COLLABORATE

Explore Main Idea and Details

The **main idea** is the most important point the author makes about a topic. **Details** tell more about the main idea.

1. **Read the text all the way through.**
   This will help you understand what the text is about.

2. **Look carefully at the pictures and charts.**

3. **See if there is a sentence that states the main idea.**
   This is often the first sentence of a paragraph. Sometimes other sentences in a paragraph can state the main idea.

4. **Now look for details.**
   Sentences with details give more information about the main idea.

 Based on the text you read, work with your class to complete the chart below.

Topic	Main Idea	Details
climate		

Investigate!

Read pages 30–39 in your Research Companion. Use your investigative skills to look for text evidence that tells you the main idea and supporting details. This chart will help you organize your notes.

Climate	Main Idea	Details
Dry and desert		
Warm summers and cold winters		
Humid summers and mild winters		
Mild seasons		

Think About It

Describe

Review your research. Based on the information you have gathered, what are the different climates found in the United States? How would you describe the climate of your community?

Write About It

Write and Cite Evidence

Write a diary entry describing how the climate in your community impacted something you have done in the past.

_____

_____

_____

_____

_____

_____

_____

_____

_____

_____

Talk About It

Explain

Share your diary entry with a partner. Then ask and answer questions about how climate where you live affects each of you.

Geography

Connect to the  EQ

Pull It Together

Think about how climate affects your community. How does this help you understand why it matters where you live?

_____

_____

_____

 Inquiry Project Notes

_____

_____

_____

_____

How Is My Community Affected by the Land and Water Around It?

Lesson Outcomes

What Am I Learning?

In this lesson, you will use your investigative skills to explore how the land and water around a community affect the people who live there.

Why Am I Learning It?

Reading and talking about the land and water around communities will help you understand your community and other communities.

How Will I Know That I Learned It?

You will be able to write a paragraph that describes the land and water around your community.

Talk About It

COLLABORATE

Look closely at the picture. What do you notice about the land and water? How would you describe the community?

Many communities, such as Poughkeepsie, NY, were built along a river.

Rivers

1 Inspect

Read the text and the quote. What river is described in the quote?

- **Circle** words you do not know.
- **Underline** words that tell how communities benefit from rivers.
- **Discuss** with a partner what the quote reveals about how Mark Twain felt about the river.

My Notes

_____

_____

_____

_____

_____

_____

_____

_____

Rivers are a very important water form to many communities. A river is a stream of fresh water that flows into another body of water. People often settle near rivers and build communities. Rivers provide transportation routes that connect cities. They also supply water for drinking, farming, and industry. Rivers offer people recreation, such as boating, swimming, and watersports. Rivers also bring tourists to a community.

Rivers in the United States are different from each other. The Los Angeles River is 51 miles long and runs through the city of Los Angeles. Flooding caused property damage in the past, so the river was paved to create a clear path. The Allegheny River is about 320 miles long. It runs through forests and farmlands in New York and Pennsylvania. The Allegheny empties into the Ohio River. The Ohio empties into the Mississippi River.

The Mississippi River is approximately 2,350 miles long. It flows from Minnesota all the way to the Gulf of Mexico. It varies from 20 feet wide to more than 11 miles wide. The speed of the water flow changes as it moves from wide parts of the river to more narrow stretches. Water flowing in the Mississippi takes about three months to flow from beginning to end.

Mark Twain is a famous author who wrote about his experiences as a steamboat pilot on the Mississippi River. A steamboat is a boat that moves with steam. Early steamboats used paddle wheels, wheels that move through water as they turn, to transport passengers and goods. Being a steamboat pilot on the Mississippi was hard work because of the changing speed and depth of the flowing water. Mark Twain's book *Life on the Mississippi* includes his thoughts about the mighty river.

PRIMARY SOURCE

In Their Words ... Mark Twain

"One who knows the Mississippi will promptly aver—not aloud, but to himself—that ten thousand River Commissions, with the mines of the world at their back, cannot tame that lawless stream, cannot curb it or confine it, cannot say to it, Go here, or Go there, and make it obey; cannot save a shore which it has sentenced; cannot bar its path with an obstruction which it will not tear down, dance over, and laugh at."

– *Life on the Mississippi*, 1883

Steamboat pilots once traveled up and down the Mississippi River.

Copyright © McGraw-Hill Education
TEXT: Twain, Mark. Life on the Mississippi. Boston: James R. Osgood & Co. 1883

2 Find Evidence

Reread the text. Circle details in text and make notes next to pictures.

Look at the photo. How do the photo and the quote help you understand what it might have been like to travel on a steamboat up and down the Mississippi River? Would you want to travel this way on the Mississippi? Why or why not?

3 Make Connections

Write Just as rivers can be valuable to a community, they can also cause problems. Write your own quote about the physical characteristics of rivers and how they might help or harm your community.

COLLABORATE

Explore Compare and Contrast

To **compare** means to tell how two or more things are alike.
To **contrast** means to tell how two or more things are different.

1. **Read the text all the way through.**
   This will help you understand what the text is about.

2. **Look for words that signal comparisons and contrasts.**
   Both, some, like, and *as* can help you find comparisons.
   But and *unlike* can help you find contrasts.

3. **Think about the details in the text and pictures.**
   Look for details that show how things are similar and
   different.

Based on the text you read, work with your class
to complete the chart below.

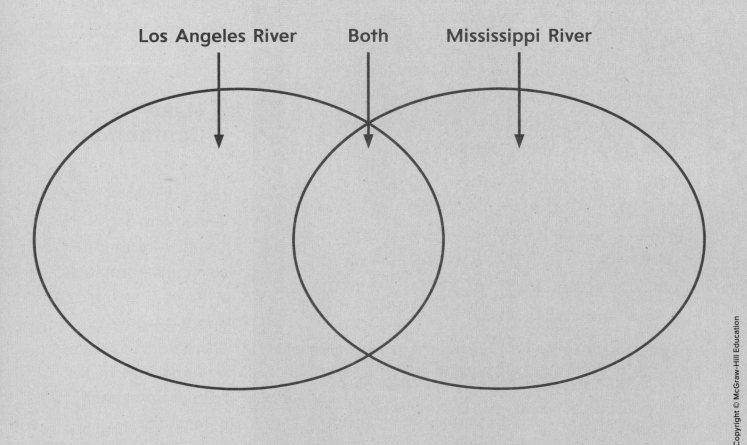

Los Angeles River   Both   Mississippi River

Investigate!

Read pages 40–49 in your Research Companion. Use your investigative skills to look for text evidence that will help you describe the land and water features for different communities. This chart will help you organize your notes.

Land (Mountain and Valley Communities) Both Water (River and Coastal Communities)

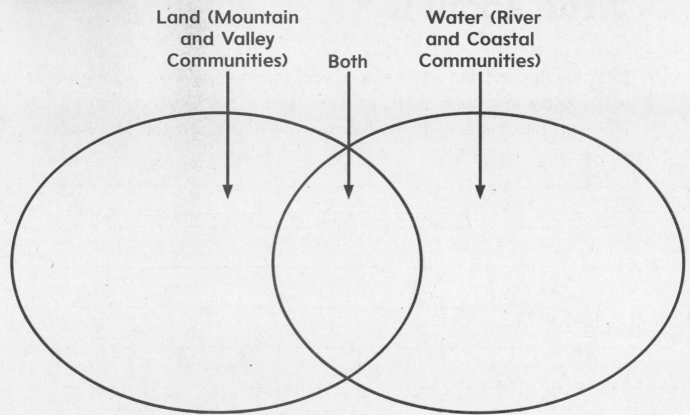

Think About It

Gather Ideas

Review your research. Think about the physical characteristics of your community.

Write About It

Write and Cite Evidence

Describe the land and water around your community. How are they similar to the land and water features you have read about? How are they different? Cite evidence from what you have read to support your answer.

_____

_____

_____

_____

_____

_____

_____

_____

_____

_____

_____

Talk About It

Explain

Share your response with a partner. Together, discuss how the physical characteristics of your community compare to those of other communities.

Geography

Connect to the

Pull It Together

How does the land and water around your community compare to other nearby communities? How does this show why where you live matters?

_____

_____

_____

_____

_____

_____

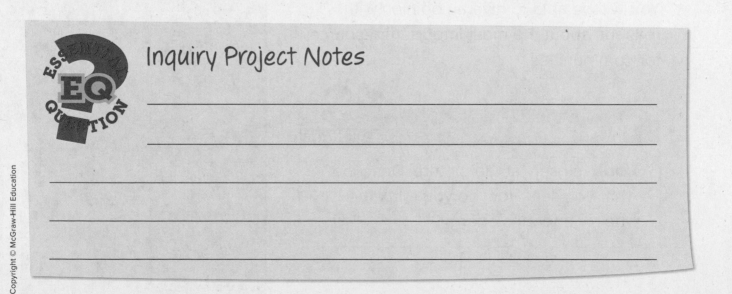

Inquiry Project Notes

_____

_____

_____

_____

Lesson 5

How Do Resources Impact a Community?

Lesson Outcomes

What Am I Learning?

In this lesson, you will use your investigative skills to explore different types of natural resources and how people use those resources.

Why Am I Learning It?

Reading and talking about how communities use land, water, and other resources will help you understand how location affects how people live in different communities.

How Will I Know That I Learned It?

You will be able to give an opinion with reasons about the most important resource for communities.

Talk About It

COLLABORATE

Look closely at the picture. Describe what you see. How do you think the wheel generates energy?

Waterwheels turn energy from moving water into power that people can use for other things.

1 Inspect

Look at the images carefully. What do you expect to read about?

- **List** three adjectives that describe what you see in the first image.
- **Identify** the three types of mines shown in the second image.
- **Circle** examples of shaft mining.
- **Underline** examples of slope mining.

My Notes

_____

_____

_____

_____

_____

_____

_____

_____

Where Does Our Energy Come From?

When you turn on a light or use a computer, you are using energy. Most energy used by machines comes from natural resources called fossil fuels. In 2017, the top three fossil fuels used in the United States were oil, natural gas, and coal. People dig wells to pump oil and natural gas up to the surface of the ground. People also dig mines to reach coal deposits. Coal is found on every continent and in many countries, but not in every community. Coal is often found in mountainous regions.

The United States has some of the largest coal deposits in the world. They are found in the Appalachian Mountains, the Rocky Mountains, and in other areas. Many communities in the United States depend on coal. They use coal to power their homes and businesses. They also sell and trade coal to other places. Coal mining is hard and dangerous work, but it shapes life in many communities.

To reach coal, miners dig hundreds, even thousands, of feet underground. They use special equipment to travel in and out of the mines.

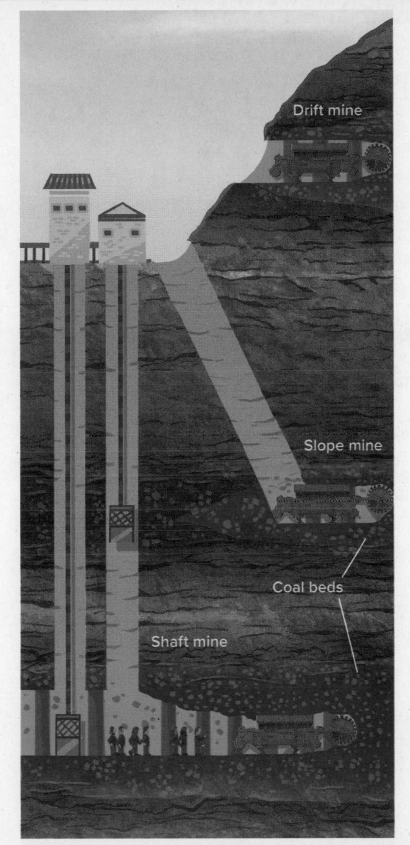

Drift mine

Slope mine

Coal beds

Shaft mine

Coal deposits can be far underground and deep within mountains. Shaft mines go straight down a long way beneath the surface. Slope and drift mines tunnel into mountainsides. Surface mining for coal, not shown here, involves removing large areas of earth.

2 Find Evidence

Underline the sentence that describes what work in a coal mine is like.

Reread How do the images support this description?

Read the captions and study the images again. How else might you describe the work done by coal miners?

3 Make Connections

Talk As you know, landforms and water impact nearby communities. How might having a mountain with coal deposits impact nearby communities?

COLLABORATE

Explore Drawing Conclusions

A **conclusion** is a judgment about events or conditions. To **draw a conclusion**, you use text clues and your own knowledge to make a judgment. This judgment might be about why something happens, how something works, or what something is like. You can also use visual clues in images, charts, graphs, and maps.

1. **Read the text and study the images.**
   This will help you understand what the text and images are about. You will draw your conclusion about the overall subject.

2. **Highlight or underline important details in the text and images.**
   Think about how these details relate to one another and to the subject.

3. **Recall what you already know about the subject.**
   Connect your knowledge to the ideas in the text and images.

4. **Ask yourself,** *What do the details and my own knowledge make me think about this subject?* Use what you have learned and what you know to draw a conclusion.

 Based on the text you read, work with your class to complete the chart below.

Text Clues	Conclusion
People dig different types of mines to reach coal in different places.	
Coal mines look dark, dirty, deep, and tight.	

Investigate!

Read pages 50–57 in your Research Companion. Use your investigative skills to look for text evidence that helps you draw conclusions about how communities use natural resources. This chart will help you organize your notes.

Text Clues	Conclusion

Think About It

Recall Details

Think about these five different resources that impact communities—land, minerals, fossil fuels, water, and climate. What makes each resource important for a community?

Write About It

Write and Cite Evidence

Of the five resources you have considered, what do you think is the most important resource for a community? Provide evidence to support your opinion. You can use the importance of the resources to your own community to help support your argument.

_____

_____

_____

_____

_____

_____

_____

_____

_____

_____

_____

Talk About It

Explain

Share your response with a partner. Compare and contrast your opinions of the most important resources for a community. Do you agree or disagree with your partner's opinion? Why?

Connect to the EQ

Pull It Together

How does the availability of resources make an impact on how people live or where people choose to live? Describe why the availability of resources matters to where we live.

_____

_____

_____

_____

 Inquiry Project Notes

_____

_____

_____

_____

_____

Why Does It Matter Where We Live?

Inquiry Project

Understanding Your Community

For this project, you will choose at least three features that make your community special. Then you will create a travel brochure about your community.

Complete Your Project

☐ Identify at least three features that make your community special.

☐ Conduct research on the features you chose.

☐ Organize what you have learned in a travel brochure.

☐ Use pictures, words, and maps to tell about your community.

Share Your Project

☐ Name the features you have chosen.

☐ Tell about each feature. Explain where it is located and why it is special to your community.

☐ Show your travel brochure. Explain each part.

☐ Answer any questions your class might have.

Reflect on Your Project

Think about the work you did in this chapter and on your project. Use the questions below to help guide your thoughts.

1. Why did you choose the features that you researched?

_____

2. How did you conduct your research? Is there anything you'd do

differently next time? _____

_____

3. How did you make sure that your sources were reliable?_____

_____

Chapter Connections

Use pictures, words, or both to reflect on what you learned in this chapter.

The most interesting thing I learned:

Something I learned from a classmate:

A connection I can make with my own life:

Exploring Planet Ava

CHARACTERS

Narrator
Captain Woods
Robb
Jane *(Robb and Susan's mother)*
Susan
Co-captain Carson

Four Explorers
1. Omar
2. Luke
3. Carla
4. Roger

Narrator: It's the year 2350. A spacecraft with men, women, and children from Earth is heading to the planet Ava. Earth and Planet Ava are very much alike. Ava has air and water, mountains, rivers, and good soil. Planet Ava has two natural resources that Earth does not have—Kottowool trees and a rare mineral called cordromite. The people from Earth are coming to farm Ava's Kottowool trees. They also want to mine its cordromite and send it back to Earth.

Captain Woods: Ladies and gentlemen, this is Captain Woods speaking. Please prepare for landing. Remain seated until I have turned off the seat belt sign.

Robb: Mom, why is this planet called Ava?

Jane: It was named after the nine-year-old girl who discovered it. She was looking through her telescope on Earth.

Robb: I can't wait to get outside.

Captain Woods: Okay, folks, we have come to a complete stop. Let's exit the spacecraft.

(The passengers exit the spaceship.)

Robb: *(pointing to the sky)* Look at the three moons!

Susan: Look! A Kottowool tree! Kottowool is strong and soft enough to make just about anything—clothes, rugs, sheets, pillows.

Robb: *(kicking a rock with his foot)* Here's some cordromite. That's enough to power my robotic flyer for a month!

Captain Woods: *(raising his voice to be heard)* Everyone, let's gather over here. *(All of the passengers gather around.)* We're going to set up some bio-houses here for now. By spring, we'll need to decide where to set up permanent housing before the big storms come. So let's get ready to explore.

Co-captain Carson: *(holding a digital tablet)* We have divided Ava into four regions. Each team will take a rover to explore one region. Look for natural resources, and be on the lookout for Kottowool trees and cordromite. Take video to share with the team. We'll meet back here tonight.

Narrator: The teams went in four different directions. At the end of the day, they gathered in the group living space.

Captain Woods: Well, Team 1, what did you find today?

Omar: In our region, there was a valley between two huge mountains. You can see a river that runs through it on our video.

Captain Woods: Good. We need water for drinking and washing. We also need it for the food we will grow.

Omar: The soil seems good for farming. The climate was comfortable, too.

Captain Woods: What about Kottowool trees?

Robb: *(disappointed)* We saw lots of trees but not many were Kottowool. We didn't find too much cordromite, either.

Captain Woods: Team 2, what did you find?

Susan: Our region was very hot and dry. It was a desert. There wasn't a drop of water or any Kottowool trees in sight.

Luke: We don't want to live there, sir.

Captain Woods: I agree. Team 3, you're next.

Jane: Our region has a coast. There's a beautiful beach, and two rivers empty into the ocean. We would never run out of water, that's for sure.

Susan: I would like to live near a beach! We could grow Kottowool trees.

Co-captain Carson: *(frowning)* What about cordromite?

Jane: We found some in one spot, but nowhere else.

Captain Woods: Team 4, what did you see?

Roger: *(excitedly)* Our region had mountains. Some had snow on top. There were forests of Kottowool, and our cordromite meter went nuts. There's one problem—water. There's probably not enough water for us to live and farm.

Captain Woods: That IS a problem. Is the soil rich?

Roger: Yes. We brought back soil samples. Take a look.

Captain Woods: What about the climate? What's it like?

Carla: *(shrugging)* It's in the mountains, so it's cool. But it's not freezing.

Captain Woods: It sounds like a great place for us. Like the first region, it has a good climate and rich soil for farming. But it also has plenty of cordromite and Kottowool trees. How do we solve the water problem?

Roger: Captain, we could build a lake to collect and store water from rain and melted snow. Then we'll have water when we need it.

Captain Woods: Roger, that's a good plan. I think we might just name our new community "Rogersville."

Talk About It

Talk Think about the town where you live. Why do you think the people who settled there thought It would be a good place to live? Do you know how it got its name? Talk with a partner about your ideas.

What Is Our Relationship With Our Environment?

In this chapter, you will explore how a community's environment affects the way people live. You will learn how people change their environment to meet their needs. You also will learn how people work together to solve problems with their environment. With a team, you will work on a chapter project to identify a problem with your community's environment. Then your team will create a plan to solve that problem.

Talk About It COLLABORATE

Talk with a partner about how people affect the environment. How does the environment affect people? Write down questions you have.

Improving the Environment

In this project, you will think of a way to improve your community's environment. Then your team will create a plan for an improvement and present it to the class.

Project Checklist

☐ **Think** about your community's environment.

☐ **Choose** one issue that your team could improve.

☐ **Conduct** research to learn more about the issue. What might cause the issue? Do other communities have this issue? How have they tried to solve it?

☐ **Create** a presentation that describes your plan to improve your community's environment. Use both words and pictures.

☐ **Present** your plan to the class.

My Research Plan

Write down any research questions you have that will help you plan your project. You can add questions as you carry out your research.

_____

_____

_____

_____

_____

Complete this chapter's Word Rater. Write notes as you learn more about each word.

atmosphere

- ☐ Know It!
- ☐ Heard It!
- ☐ Don't Know It!

My Notes

_____

_____

_____

deforestation

- ☐ Know It!
- ☐ Heard It!
- ☐ Don't Know It!

My Notes

_____

_____

_____

ecosystem

- ☐ Know It!
- ☐ Heard It!
- ☐ Don't Know It!

My Notes

_____

_____

_____

endangered

- ☐ Know It!
- ☐ Heard It!
- ☐ Don't Know It!

My Notes

_____

_____

_____

extinct

- ☐ Know It!
- ☐ Heard It!
- ☐ Don't Know It!

My Notes

_____

_____

_____

habitat

My Notes

- ☐ Know It!
- ☐ Heard It!
- ☐ Don't Know It!

_____

_____

_____

hydroelectric dam

My Notes

- ☐ Know It!
- ☐ Heard It!
- ☐ Don't Know It!

_____

_____

_____

natural disaster

My Notes

- ☐ Know It!
- ☐ Heard It!
- ☐ Don't Know It!

_____

_____

_____

ozone layer

My Notes

- ☐ Know It!
- ☐ Heard It!
- ☐ Don't Know It!

_____

_____

_____

technology

My Notes

- ☐ Know It!
- ☐ Heard It!
- ☐ Don't Know It!

_____

_____

_____

How Does the Environment Change the Way People Live?

Lesson Outcomes

What Am I Learning?

In this lesson, you are going to use your investigative skills to explore how people are affected by their surroundings.

Why Am I Learning It?

Reading and talking about different environments and resources will help you understand how people adapt to their surroundings.

How Will I Know That I Learned It?

You will be able to list resources from your environment that you could use for food, shelter, tools, and transportation.

Talk About It

COLLABORATE

Look at the photograph of a willow tree and read the quotation on the next page. How does Jane Dumas say we use willow trees? Can you think of any other things made from plants?

PRIMARY SOURCE

In Their Words... Jane Dumas

"A lot of plants have a lot of meaning to a lot of people. The willow gives us clothes to wear, the wood to build our homes and aspirin comes from the willow."

—Jane Dumas

Look Compare the two images. What do you think this text will be about?

Circle words that tell when something happened or is happening.

Underline clues that tell you:

- for what purposes people use natural resources
- how people gathered seeds long ago
- how people can harvest seeds now

My Notes

_____

_____

_____

_____

_____

Using Natural Resources: Then and Now

Long ago, Native Americans adapted to their environment. Their food, shelter, transportation, and tools were shaped by the natural resources around them. They learned which plants were safe to eat and how to gather them. They knew how to fish and hunt.

Today, people still adapt to their environment. We also use natural resources for food, shelter, transportation, and tools. Modern technology has changed the way we use our resources, though. Farmers use modern tools to plant, irrigate, and harvest crops.

Before modern machines, people gathered seeds by hand. They had to separate the seeds from the rest of the plant. Then they had to remove the hard shells from the seeds. It took a long time and a lot of work to produce a small amount of edible seeds.

Instead of harvesting seeds by hand, farmers now use powerful machines. This seed harvester automatically picks, separates, and cleans the seeds. It can harvest more than three bushels of seeds per second!

Even though today's tools are different from long ago, people still adapt to their environment by using the land around them.

A Native American woman gathering seeds

A modern seed harvesting machine

2 Find Evidence

Look The photo shows a woman gathering seeds. How is she using the resources around her? What can you tell about the tools she is using?

3 Make Connections

Talk What are the differences COLLABORATE between using machinery to harvest seeds and harvesting seeds by hand? Why do you think using machines is more important today than it was 150 years ago?

Explore Making Inferences

When you read, you often **make inferences** about the text.
An **inference** is a decision you make about the meaning of the
text. To make an inference:

1. **Read the text once all the way through.**
   This will help you understand what the text is about.

2. **Think about what you read.**
   An author may not always tell you everything. What
   questions do you have?

3. **Think about what you already know about this topic.**

4. **Make a decision about the text.**
   Base your decision on what you know and what you read.

 Based on the text you read, work with your class to
complete the chart below.

Text Clues and What I Already Know	Inferences
It took a long time and a lot of work to produce a small amount of edible seeds. I know:	This text means:

Investigate!

Read pages 66–71 in your Research Companion. Use your investigative skills to look for text evidence that tells you how people adapt to their environment. This chart will help you organize your notes.

Text Clues and What I Already Know	Inferences
In different regions, Native Americans made boats out of tall grasses, hollowed-out tree trunks, or animal skins. I know:	This text means:
People in New York can buy potatoes from Idaho and oranges from Florida. I know:	This text means:
The photograph shows a house on stilts and the tells about houses with steep roofs. I know:	The photo and text mean:

Think About It

Reflect

Imagine that there are no stores to sell you the things you need. What resources from your environment would you use for food, shelter, tools, and transportation in the region where you live?

Write About It

Identify

Write a list telling which natural resources from your region you would use for food, shelter, tools, and transportation.

_____

_____

_____

_____

_____

_____

_____

_____

_____

_____

_____

_____

Talk About It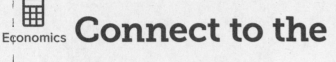

Consider Different Ideas

Share your list with a partner. How do your ideas for using natural resources differ?

Connect to the

Explain

How has technology changed the way people adapt to the environment?

_____

_____

_____

_____

_____

_____

Inquiry Project Notes

_____

_____

_____

_____

_____

Lesson Outcomes

What Am I Learning?

In this lesson, you are going to use your investigative skills to explore how people have changed the environment to survive and to support their communities.

Why Am I Learning It?

Reading and talking about how people affect the environment will help you understand the relationship between humans, human activity, and plant and animal life.

How Will I Know That I Learned It?

You will be able to write a paragraph describing how people have changed their environment.

Talk About It

COLLABORATE

Look closely at the picture and caption. What kind of work do you see people doing? What do you think it took to build the Erie Canal? How do you think that work may have changed the landscape?

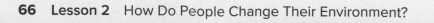

The Erie Canal is a human-made waterway in New York. It was completed in 1825. The canal was used for moving people and goods from the Great Lakes to the Atlantic Ocean.

Changing a Waterway

1 Inspect

Read the title and look at the image. What do you think this text will be about?

Circle the names of natural waterways.

Draw a box around the names of human-made waterways.

Discuss with a partner the waterways found in your community.

My Notes

_____

_____

_____

_____

_____

_____

_____

_____

_____

In the 1800s, Chicago grew quickly. Many people and businesses produced a lot of waste. This waste polluted the Chicago River and flowed to Lake Michigan. The lake supplied the city's drinking water. It also supplied fish. Many people started to get sick from the lake water.

People in Chicago wanted to stop pollution from reaching the lake. They decided to reverse, or change the direction of, the Chicago River's flow. To do this, pumps pushed water from the river to a canal. The job was too big for those

The Chicago River was changed so it flows away from its mouth.

pumps, though. So workers built a new canal called the Chicago Sanitary and Ship Canal. The Chicago River flowed through this second canal to the Des Plaines River.

The Chicago Sanitary and Ship Canal helped solve one problem but caused others. Fewer people in Chicago got sick, but wastewater flowed to other communities. Reversing the river also meant that water flowed from the Lake Michigan to the Mississippi River. As a result the **habitat**, or home, of plants and animals changed. It also caused new sources of flooding.

2 Find Evidence

Underline words and phrases that explain:

- how people change land and water
- why people change land and water

Reread What are some of the effects of changing a waterway?

3 Make Connections

Talk How do canals help people? Explain the purpose of canals to a friend.

Draw a picture showing one way your community has changed the environment. Show one benefit and one drawback of that change.

Explore Cause and Effect

An **effect** is something that happens. A **cause** is why it happens. As you read, look out for something that causes another thing to happen.

1. **Read the text all the way through.**
   This will help you understand what the text is about.

2. **Understand how causes and effects are related.**
   A cause happens before an effect. As you read, look for clue words that tell the order in which the events happened. Sometimes a cause may have many effects.

3. **Watch for words that signal a cause or effect.**
   Words such as *so, since, because,* and *as a result* often indicate a cause-and-effect relationship.

4. **Ask yourself: *What happened? Why did it happen?***
   The answer to *Why did it happen?* is a cause.

COLLABORATE
Based on the text you read, work with your class to complete the chart below.

Cause	Effect
People want a waterway to travel across New York.	
Wastewater from the Chicago River pollutes Lake Michigan.	
	Chicago builds a canal from the Chicago River to the Des Plaines River.

Investigate!

Read pages 72–77 in your Research Companion. Use your investigative skills to look for text evidence that tells you about things that happened (effects) and why they happened (causes). This chart will help you organize your notes.

Cause	Effect

Think About It

Explain

Review your research. Based on the information you have gathered, why do you think people change things in their environment?

Write About It

Write and Cite Evidence

Use what you read to describe an example of how people affect the environment. Then describe an example of how changes to the environment affect people.

_____

_____

_____

_____

_____

_____

_____

_____

_____

_____

_____

Talk About It

Express Your Opinion

Talk to your partner about changes in your community that have affected the environment. Which do you think have been most helpful and why? Which do you think have caused new challenges and why?

Geography

Connect to the

Describe and Predict

Think about how your community has changed over time and how it might change in the future. Draw and label three pictures that show physical and human-made features in your community.

1. What do you think your community looked like before people settled there?

2. What does your community look like today?

3. How might your community look in the future?

Inquiry Project Notes

_____

_____

_____

_____

_____

_____

Lesson 3
How Do We Meet Environmental Challenges?

Lesson Outcomes

What Am I Learning?

In this lesson, you are going to use your investigative skills to explore how people solve problems related to the environment.

Why Am I Learning It?

Reading and talking about solving problems with the environment will help you understand how nature and people impact the environment.

How Will I Know That I Learned It?

You will be able to write a paragraph suggesting steps to solve a problem in the environment.

Talk About It
COLLABORATE

Look closely at the picture. What do you notice? Why do you think plastic can be dangerous to ocean life?

Pollution, like these plastic rings for cans or bottles, can harm ocean life.

Rachel Carson and the Environment

Rachel Carson was a biologist and nature writer. A biologist studies plant and animal life. Her mother loved nature. She inspired Rachel's interest in the environment. In the 1930s, Carson created radio programs about sea life for the United States Bureau of Fisheries. Later, she wrote pamphlets on protecting natural resources. Then she began to write books about the environment. In 1962, she wrote the book *Silent Spring*. The book told how the overuse of pesticides was harming the environment. A pesticide is a substance used to kill insects that harm plants and crops. Pesticides can also cause animals and people to become ill. In *Silent Spring*, Carson said that the government and scientists working in agriculture needed to take better care of the environment. To solve this, she wanted rules that would protect the environment and people from these dangerous chemicals. Many pesticides are no longer used today because of Rachel Carson.

PRIMARY SOURCE

In Their Words... Rachel Carson

"Only within the moment of time represented by the present century has one species—man—acquired significant power to alter the nature of his world."

—from *Silent Spring*

Copyright © McGraw-Hill Education
TEXT: Rachel Carson. Silent Spring. New York: Houghton-Mifflin Harcourt, 1962.

Rachel Carson's book sparked national interest in the environment. In 1970, the first Earth Day was held. It addresses some problems in the environment. It led people to clean up pollution, to recycle, and to conserve, or protect, the environment. The environmental movement

Rachel Carson

had begun. One solution to the problem of pollution was that people started using "green," or sustainable, products. A sustainable product does not harm Earth or the environment. It helps conserve it for the future. Another solution was that the government passed laws such as the Clean Water Act, the Safe Drinking Water Act, and the Endangered Species Act. Carson is often referred to as the "Mother of the Environmental Movement."

Rachel Carson wanted to preserve natural environments like this spring.

2 Find Evidence

Reread the Primary Source quote. Who did Rachel Carson say is causing the problems with the environment? Why do you think she said this?

Think about the phrase "moment of time." What does the phrase mean? Is it still happening? Name a word that has a similar meaning.

3 Make Connections

Talk Think about the ocean shown in the photo on page 75. How could people solve the problem shown in the photo?

Explore Problem and Solution

A **problem** is a difficult situation. A **solution** is a way to solve a problem.

1. **Read the text all the way through.**
   This will help you identify problems that are being described.

2. **Find any steps that show how the problem might be solved.**
   Look for details that explain what was done to help solve the problem.

3. **Find any solutions that are provided.**
   Look for ways that the problem was solved.

 Based on the text you read, work with your class to complete the chart below.

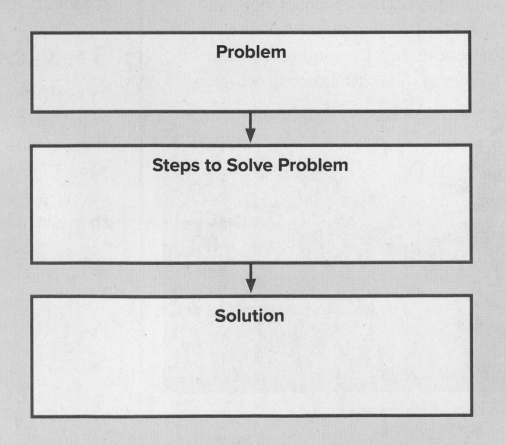

Problem

↓

Steps to Solve Problem

↓

Solution

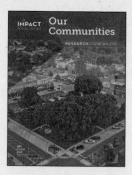

Investigate!

Read pages 78–87 in your Research Companion. Use your investigative skills to look for information about problems, steps to solve problems, and solutions. This chart will help you organize your notes.

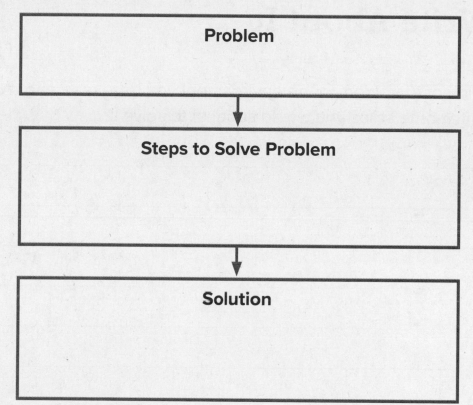

Problem

Steps to Solve Problem

Solution

Think About It

Examine
Review your research. What are some problems related to the environment?
How have some of these problems been solved?

Write About It

Write and Cite Evidence
Think of a problem in the environment you have read about or heard about.
Write some steps you would suggest to solve it.

_____

_____

_____

_____

_____

_____

_____

_____

_____

_____

_____

Talk About It

Explain

Share your response with a partner. Together, discuss the steps suggested to solve the problem. What step do you think is most important? Why?

Geography

Connect to the

Pull It Together

Think about how and why people solve problems with the environment. How have these solutions affected the environment?

_____

_____

_____

_____

_____

_____

 Inquiry Project Notes

_____

_____

_____

_____

What Is Our Relationship With Our Environment?

Inquiry Project

Improving the Environment

For this project, you will present a plan to improve the environment in your community.

Complete Your Project

- ☐ Identify a way to improve your community's environment.
- ☐ Conduct research about that issue.
- ☐ Create a presentation to describe your plan.
- ☐ Use pictures and words to tell about the planned improvement.

Share Your Project

- ☐ Name the plan.
- ☐ Explain why this plan will improve your environment.
- ☐ Show pictures that support your plan.
- ☐ Answer any questions your class might have.

Reflect on Your Project

Think about the work you did in this chapter and on your project. Use the questions below to help guide your thoughts.

1. Why did you choose the improvement that you researched?

_____

2. How did you conduct your research? Is there anything you'd do differently next time? _____

_____

3. How did you make sure that your sources were reliable? _____

_____

Chapter Connections

Use pictures, words, or both to reflect on what you learned in this chapter.

The most interesting thing I learned:

Something I learned from a classmate:

A connection I can make with my own life:

People and Communities

What Makes a Community Unique?

You have learned about physical features that are found in communities, such as landforms, bodies of water, and the climate. In this chapter, you will explore cultural features, such as art, music, and dance. You will read about how these features make communities special. With a team, you will plan a holiday or festival that celebrates the different cultures of the students at your school.

Talk About It COLLABORATE

Talk with your partner about the questions you have about culture in the United States and the world.

Planning a Cultural Event

In this project, you will work with a team to create a plan for a holiday or festival your school could hold to celebrate the different cultures of your classmates.

Project Checklist

☐ **Think** of the different cultures of your classmates.

☐ **Conduct** research to learn more about these cultures.

☐ **Choose** ways to express at least three of these cultures, such as through events, dances, art, or stories.

☐ **Create** a plan for a holiday or festival to celebrate these cultures at your school.

☐ **Share** your plan with the rest of the class.

My Research Plan

Write down any research questions you have that will help you plan your project. You can add questions as you carry out your research.

_____

_____

_____

_____

_____

_____

Explore Words

Complete this chapter's Word Rater. Write notes as you learn more about each word.

apartheid

My Notes

☐ Know It!

☐ Heard It!

☐ Don't Know It!

_____

_____

_____

artifact

My Notes

☐ Know It!

☐ Heard It!

☐ Don't Know It!

_____

_____

_____

citizen

My Notes

☐ Know It!

☐ Heard It!

☐ Don't Know It!

_____

_____

_____

culture

My Notes

☐ Know It!

☐ Heard It!

☐ Don't Know It!

_____

_____

_____

ethnic groups

My Notes

☐ Know It!

☐ Heard It!

☐ Don't Know It!

_____

_____

_____

folktale

☐ Know It!
☐ Heard It!
☐ Don't Know It!

My Notes

_____

_____

_____

heritage

☐ Know It!
☐ Heard It!
☐ Don't Know It!

My Notes

_____

_____

_____

oral tradition

☐ Know It!
☐ Heard It!
☐ Don't Know It!

My Notes

_____

_____

_____

pioneer

☐ Know It!
☐ Heard It!
☐ Don't Know It!

My Notes

_____

_____

_____

tolerance

☐ Know It!
☐ Heard It!
☐ Don't Know It!

My Notes

_____

_____

_____

Lesson Outcomes

What Am I Learning?

In this lesson, you will use your investigative skills to explore what *culture* means and how cultures around the world are different and similar.

Why Am I Learning It?

Reading and talking about cultures will help you make connections between people and places.

How Will I Know That I Learned It?

You will be able to write a paragraph that defines *culture* and explains why culture matters.

Talk About It

Look closely at the sculpture. What does the picture lead you to believe *culture* might mean?

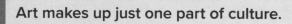

Art makes up just one part of culture.

How Cultures Form

1 Inspect

Read the article and look at the images. How do the images help you understand the text?

Circle words you do not know.

Underline words you have already learned.

List parts of culture.

My Notes

_____

_____

_____

_____

_____

_____

_____

_____

_____

_____

When people began forming communities, they also developed cultures. *Culture* means the values, beliefs, and other ways of life shared by a group of people.

Cultures can be as big as a world culture linked by trade and technology. Cultures can also be as small as a family group. Some communities and nations have one main culture. They might have a few smaller cultures. Others, like the United States, are home to many different cultures.

Many culture groups have come to the United States over time. Native Americans were the earliest people to live here. They formed unique, or special, cultures across the continent. Their environments shaped their cultures. People in the east, like the Cherokee, learned to make clothing from plants that grew around them. People further north learned to make clothes from the animals that lived there. Some cultures used plant dyes to decorate themselves and their goods. Others used stones, shells, or other resources found nearby.

Clothing, music, jewelry, tools, and food all express, or show, culture.

Later, people from Asia, Europe, and other parts of the world also came to the Americas. African people were brought as enslaved people. They, too, brought their cultures. Then and now, culture groups work to preserve, or keep, their cultures alive. They do so through shared activities. These include art, music, stories, games, celebrations, and religious gatherings.

2 Find Evidence

Reread Where are cultures found?

Highlight ways that environment affects culture.

Describe How do people preserve culture?

3 Make Connections

Talk Think about the cultural activities shown in the photographs on this page. Turn back to page 89. How do the photographs on both pages show what culture is?

COLLABORATE

Explore Summarizing

To **summarize** means to retell something in your own words.
A **summary** tells the main idea and a few important details.

1. **Read the text and look at any pictures and maps.**
   Ask yourself: *What is this about?* This will help you understand the topic.

2. **Look for main ideas and details.**
   Titles, labels, images, and words on the page will help you understand what you are learning.

3. **Say in a few words what it is about.**
   Explain it in your own words. What does this section teach you?

 Based on the text you read, work with your class to complete the chart below. Then summarize the information in the text and the images.

Topic	Main Idea	Details
The topic is culture, what it is, and how it forms.		

Summary: _____

_____

_____

_____

_____

Investigate!

Read pages 96–101 in your Research Companion. Use your investigative skills to look for evidence that helps you understand what the topic of each section of text is. The evidence will include main ideas and details. This chart will help you organize your notes.

Topic	Main Idea	Details

Summary:

_____

_____

_____

Think About It

Gather Evidence

Review your research. Based on the information you have gathered, how do you think culture affects communities?

Write About It

Write and Cite Evidence

What is culture? What do you think about when you describe the culture of a community? Use information from the texts to explain your response.

_____

_____

_____

_____

_____

_____

_____

_____

_____

_____

_____

Talk About It

COLLABORATE

Explain

Share your response with a partner. Together, discuss different culture groups that exist in your community. Describe how those groups show and preserve their cultures.

Geography

Connect to the

Pull It Together

Why is culture important to your community? List three ideas to share with others.

1. _____

   _____

2. _____

   _____

   _____

3. _____

   _____

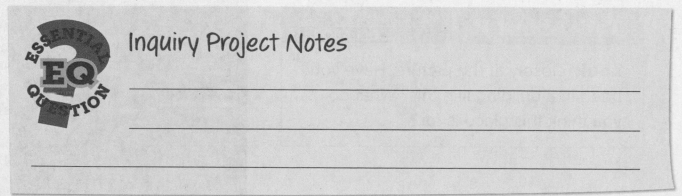

Inquiry Project Notes

_____

_____

_____

Lesson 2

How Do People Express Their Culture?

Lesson Outcomes

What Am I Learning?

In this lesson, you will use your investigative skills to find out how people and groups in the community express their cultures.

Why Am I Learning It?

Reading and talking about how communities show their diverse cultures will help you understand how people shape communities over time.

How Will I Know That I Learned It?

You will be able to write a news report showing how two people or groups in your community express their cultures.

Talk About It

COLLABORATE

Look closely at the picture. Have you been in a building like this? What do you think this place is for?

People show their cultures through dance, music, and plays.

1 Inspect

Read Look at the title and the images. What do you think this text will be about?

Circle words you do not know.

Underline clues that tell you:

- what folktales and folksongs are
- why they matter

My Notes

_____

_____

_____

_____

_____

_____

_____

_____

_____

The Story of Johnny Appleseed

Have you heard a song or a story about Johnny Appleseed? Appleseed is an American folk hero. His good deeds are the subject of folktales. A deed is something you do. A folktale is a story handed down over the years.

According to folktales, Appleseed was a friendly man who walked across parts of the United States planting apple trees. He had very few belongings and walked barefoot. He wore a pan for a hat, a coffee sack for a shirt, and ragged pants. As he traveled, he scattered apple seeds across the land.

The story of Johnny Appleseed is based on the life of John Chapman. Chapman lived in the United States more than one hundred years ago.

Born in Massachusetts, Chapman worked in an apple orchard at an early age. An orchard is a tree farm. As a teenager, Chapman traveled west. On the way, he bought land and planted apple trees. Like Appleseed, he gave away many seeds and young trees to pioneers. Pioneers were early Americans who settled in wilderness areas. Unlike Appleseed, Chapman owned land and sold his seeds and trees to make money. Chapman helped many farmers in Pennsylvania, Ohio, and Indiana get started. Both Chapman and Appleseed were known for their kindness to people and to animals.

Today, communities from Massachusetts to California hold festivals to celebrate Johnny Appleseed.

The real John Chapman sold many seeds and trees to pioneers.

2 Find Evidence

Reread the text and captions. What parts of the story of Johnny Appleseed are based on the life of Chapman? What are made up?

3 Make Connections

Talk Why do you think people make folktales out of true stories?

Explore Compare and Contrast

To **compare** is to tell how things are alike.

To **contrast** is to tell how things are different.

To **compare** and **contrast** two or more people, places, or things:

1. **Read the text all the way through.**
   This will help you understand what the text is about.

2. **Look for words that signal a comparison or a contrast.**
   Words such as *like, alike, same,* and *both* show comparison.
   Words such as *unlike* and *different* show contrast.

3. **Identify two or more people, places, or things being compared.**
   Words that show comparison and contrast often connect two or more people, places, or things in a text.

4. **Ask:** ***How are these people or things alike? How are they different?***
   Make a list or take notes.

Based on the text you read, work with your class to complete the diagram below.

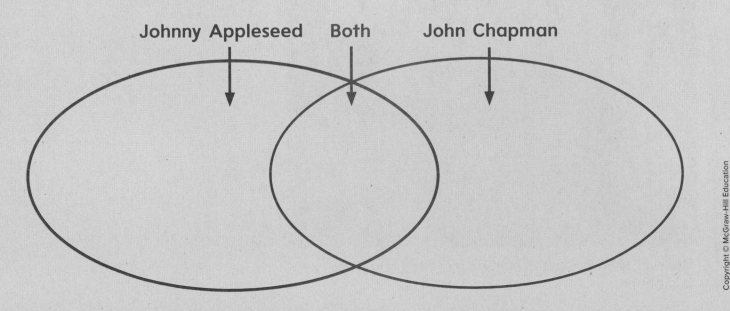

Johnny Appleseed   Both   John Chapman

Investigate!

Read pages 102–107 in your Research Companion. Use your investigative skills to look for text evidence that tells you how two groups express their cultures. This diagram will help you organize your notes.

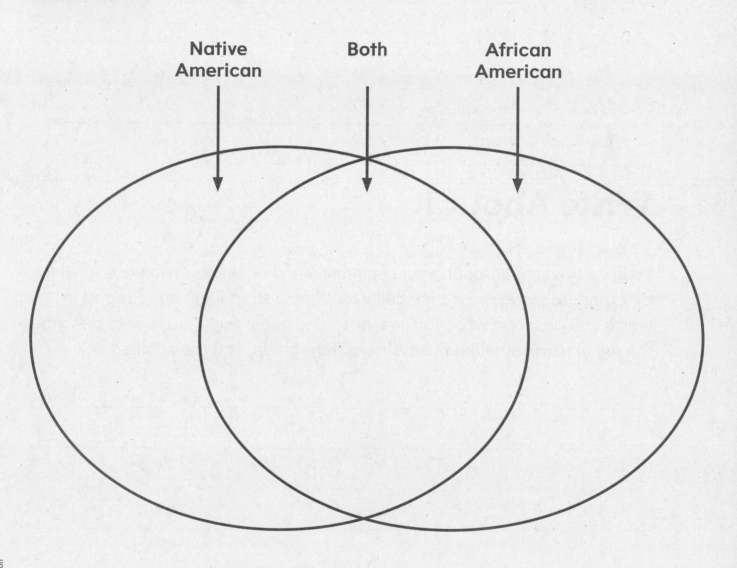

Native American   Both   African American

Think About It

Gather Evidence

How do different groups express their cultures?

_____

_____

_____

_____

_____

Write About It

Local News Report

Imagine traveling through your community and observing two ways in which different groups express their cultures. Write a short local news report in which you describe what you see, hear, and experience. Be sure to describe the location in your community, the culture group, and the events.

_____

_____

_____

_____

_____

_____

Talk About It

Explain

Share your news story with a partner. Together, discuss how different groups of people in your community express their cultures.

Geography

Connect to the

Pull It Together

How do the expressions of culture in your community make your community unique?

_____

_____

_____

_____

_____

_____

 Inquiry Project Notes

_____

_____

_____

_____

Lesson Outcomes

What Am I Learning?

In this lesson, you will use your investigative skills to look at the history of immigrants in the United States and what they have added to American life.

Why Am I Learning It?

Reading and talking about immigrants will help you understand how their contributions help make the United States a strong and diverse nation.

How Will I Know That I Learned It?

You will be able to write a newspaper article describing ways in which immigrants have enriched your community.

Talk About It

COLLABORATE

Read the quotation on the next page. What do you think the poem means? Who is the writer talking to in the poem? How do you know?

. . . "Give me your tired, your poor,

Your huddled masses yearning to breathe free,

The wretched refuse of your teeming shore.

Send these, the homeless, tempest-tost to me,

I lift my lamp beside the golden door!"

—*from* "The New Colossus"
by Emma Lazarus

The Statue of Liberty on Liberty Island in
New York Harbor

1 Inspect

Read the title. What do you think this text will be about?

Circle words you do not know.

Underline words and phrases that the author uses to describe Ellis Island.

My Notes

_____

_____

_____

_____

_____

_____

_____

_____

_____

_____

Ellis Island: Gateway to a New Life

During the 1800s, millions of immigrants arrived in the United States. They came to America seeking work, freedom, and a safe place to live. Toward the end of the 1800s, so many immigrants arrived here each year that some states had a hard time keeping track of the new arrivals. As a result, the US government made a change. In 1890, President Benjamin Harrison chose Ellis Island as the site of the first federal immigration station.

Ellis Island sits in New York Harbor. After a weeks-long journey by ship, new immigrants from Europe would spot the Statue of Liberty. They knew they had arrived in their new land. For most of them, the first stop would be Ellis Island.

Copyright © McGraw-Hill Education
PHOTO: Ron Chapple Stock/Alamy Stock Photo

Inside the Ellis Island station, immigrants waited in long lines to be inspected. These new arrivals had to present official papers showing who they were and where they came from. Immigrants were also examined for illnesses or diseases. For many, this process could be scary and uncomfortable. Then the immigrants were allowed to enter the country.

Ellis Island operated from 1892 to 1954. During that time, more than 12 million immigrants passed through its doors. At its busiest, more than 5,000 people entered the United States through Ellis Island each day.

The immigration station was crowded and was not always a pleasant place to be. But it was the gateway to a new and hopefully better life. Ellis Island became a powerful symbol of the immigrant experience.

2 Find Evidence

Reread How was Ellis Island both a positive and a negative experience for immigrants?

Underline one good thing and one bad thing about arriving as an immigrant at Ellis Island.

3 Make Connections

Talk about the reasons why an immigrant family might choose to come to the United States today. Does the poem on page 105 still describe those reasons? Why or why not? Explain your answer.

The Statue of Liberty on Liberty Island and the immigration center on Ellis Island in New York Harbor

Explore Point of View

An author's **point of view** is how he or she feels about the main topic of the text. The author may feel positive, negative, or somewhere in between (neutral). Sometimes, an author will say clearly how he or she feels. Other times, you need to look carefully at the words the author uses to describe the topic in order to recognize the point of view.

1. **Read the text all the way through.**
   This will help you understand the main topic of the text.

2. **Look for words, phrases, and sentences that describe the topic.**
   These details are clues that will help reveal the author's point of view.

3. **Make a decision about the author's point of view.**
   Base your decision on the words and phrases the author uses to describe the topic. Does the author use mostly negative words, mostly positive words, or a mixture of both?

COLLABORATE Based on the text you read, work with your class to complete the chart with details about Ellis Island.

Details

↓

Author's Point of View

Investigate!

Read pages 108–115 in your Research Companion. Use your investigative skills to look for text evidence that tells you the author's point of view about what immigrants add to a community. This chart will help you organize your notes.

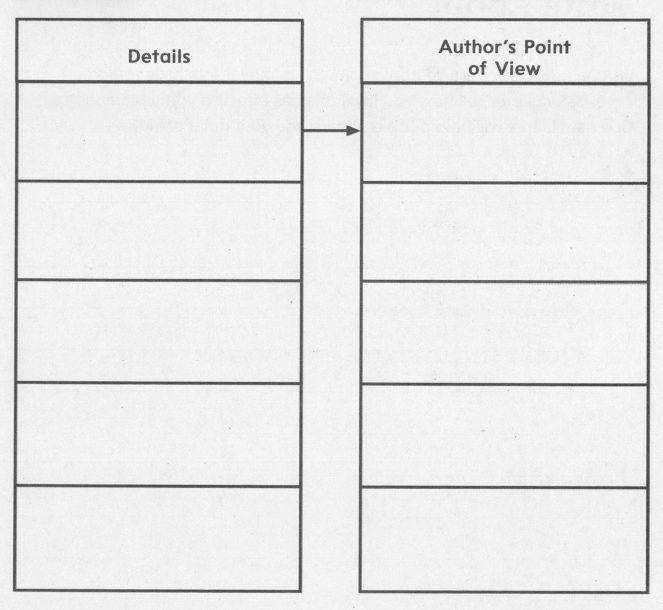

Details	Author's Point of View

Think About It

Gather Evidence

Review your research. Based on the information you have gathered, what contributions have immigrants made to American culture?

Write About It

Point of View

Write a newspaper article about something immigrants have added to American culture. Tell how you think this has affected your community. Use details that will help people understand your point of view.

_____

_____

_____

_____

_____

_____

_____

_____

_____

_____

Talk About It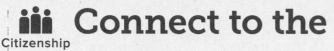

Explain

Share your newspaper article with a partner. How does your partner know what your point of view is from reading your article?

Citizenship

Connect to the

Look at Our Community

How have you experienced other cultures in your community? Think about foods you have eaten, events you have attended, and people you have met. How do they make your community unique?

_____

_____

_____

_____

_____

Inquiry Project Notes

_____

_____

_____

_____

Lesson 4

What Can Comparing Different Communities Tell Us About Global Cultures?

Lesson Outcomes

What Am I Learning?

In this lesson, you will use your investigative skills to compare and contrast cultures in two different countries.

Why Am I Learning It?

Reading and talking about different cultures help you understand people's lifestyles, traditions, holidays, and other aspects of culture.

How Will I Know That I Learned It?

You will be able to write a paragraph that compares and contrasts cultures and offer an opinion about what people can learn from other cultures.

Mapungubwe Cultural Landscape in South Africa

Talk About It

COLLABORATE

Look closely at the photos. What do you notice about each of these images? How are they similar? How are they different?

Machu Picchu in Peru

1 Inspect

Read the title. What do you think this text will be about?

Underline words or phrases that tell about the Inca civilization.

Circle words or phrases that tell about the Mapungubwe Cultural Landscape.

Discuss with a partner what you notice about the different artifacts.

My Notes

_____

_____

_____

_____

_____

_____

_____

Cultural Artifacts

An **artifact** is an object that was used by people in the past. The artifacts pictured below are from the Inca civilization of ancient Peru. This civilization was the largest empire in the Americas at the time. The Inca were known for creating new farming and building methods. They built the city of Machu Picchu without using sand or cement, and without the help of the wheel. Long ago, Machu Picchu was abandoned. No one knows why this happened, but it might have been the result of disease.

These tools and pottery are artifacts found in the ancient Inca city of Machu Picchu. They were rediscovered in 1911.

The artifact below is from the Mapungubwe Cultural Landscape. Mapungubwe was a large kingdom in southern Africa. Some of the people who lived there were gold and ivory traders. Others were successful farmers. However, the kingdom was abandoned in the fourteenth century. It is believed that climate change caused the people to leave the kingdom. The Mapungubwe Cultural Landscape is preserved so people can see the remains of this civilization.

This rhinoceros artifact from the Mapungubwe Cultural Landscape is made of gold foil. It was found buried with a king.

2 Find Evidence

Reread What was unique about the Inca and the Mapungubwe Cultural Landscape? What was the same about their cultures? Look for details that show these differences and similarities.

Look at the captions. What conclusions can you draw about each artifact? How was each artifact used? Was the purpose similar or different? Why?

3 Make Connections

Talk What comparisons can you make between these cultures based on their artifacts?

Connect to Now How do these artifacts compare to objects that are important to you?

Explore Compare and Contrast

To **compare** means to tell how two or more things are alike.
To **contrast** means to tell how two or more things are different.

1. **Read the text all the way through.**
   This will help you understand what the text is about.

2. **Look for words that signal comparisons and contrasts.**
   Both, some, like, and *as* can help you find comparisons.
   But and *unlike* can help you find contrasts.

3. **Think about the details in the text and pictures.**
   Look for details that show how things are similar and how things are different.

  Based on the text you read, work with your class to complete the chart below.

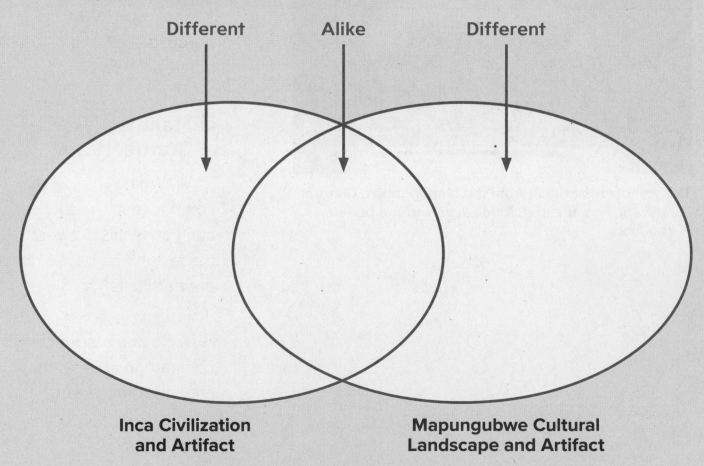

Different   Alike   Different

Inca Civilization
and Artifact

Mapungubwe Cultural
Landscape and Artifact

Investigate!

Read pages 116–125 in your Research Companion. Use your investigative skills to look for text evidence that compares and contrasts the different cultures of Peru and South Africa. This chart will help you organize your notes.

Different **Alike** **Different**

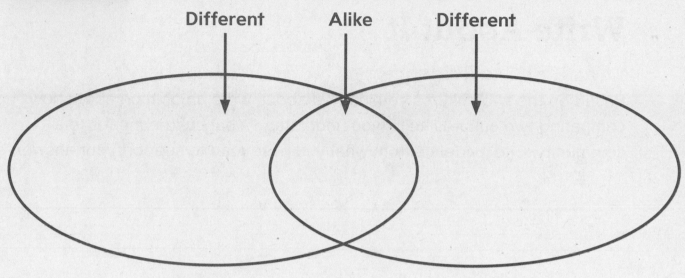

Peru   South Africa

Think About It

Gather Evidence

Review your research. Compare and contrast the cultures you learned about. What do you think are the most important things people can learn from a culture?

Write About It

Write and Cite Evidence

Based on the two cultures you learned about, write an opinion about how comparing two cultures helps you understand what culture means to a community. Cite evidence from what you have read to support your answer.

_____

_____

_____

_____

_____

_____

_____

_____

_____

_____

Talk About It

Explain

Share your opinion with a partner. Together, discuss some important things people can learn from a culture and why they are important.

Geography

Connect to the

Pull It Together

Think about what the cultures of Peru and South Africa tell about culture. In what ways do their cultures show how cultures make a community unique?

_____

_____

_____

_____

_____

_____

Inquiry Project Notes

_____

_____

_____

_____

Lesson 5
What Connects Communities Throughout the World?

Lesson Outcomes

What Am I Learning?

In this lesson, you will use your investigative skills to explore how communities around the world are connected to one another.

Why Am I Learning It?

Reading and talking about ways that communities are connected will help you understand ways that your own community is connected to the world.

How Will I Know That I Learned It?

You will be able to describe how these connections change cultures.

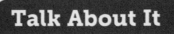

Talk About It

COLLABORATE

Look closely at the picture. What do you see? How can this connect communities?

Railroad tracks connect communities that are distant from one another.

A Railroad from Sea to Shining Sea

On May 10, 1869, two railroad engines faced one another in Utah. The transcontinental railroad was one link away from joining the Atlantic and Pacific coasts. When it was finished, people would be able to ride a train from Washington, D.C. to San Francisco, a 2,800-mile journey.

The train engine from the west belonged to the Central Pacific Railroad. This company's line began in Sacramento, California, and crossed the Sierra Nevada. Building a railroad through the mountains was difficult and dangerous. Rock had to be blasted away to make the road. Fifteen tunnels were built through rock. Most of this hard work was done by men who came from China.

The train engine from the east belonged to the Union Pacific Railroad. This company's line began near Omaha, Nebraska. The tracks crossed the Great Plains. The ties, steel rails, spikes, food, and other supplies were brought in by train. Most of the

Railroad officials pounded this spike into the ground to show that a transportation line joined the East and West Coasts of the United States and all the communities between. How did this change life for people in the United States?

Locomotives and crews from the two railroad companies face each other at Promontory Point, Utah.

Union Pacific Railroad workers were Civil War veterans, Chinese immigrants, or Irish immigrants. Native Americans did not want a train going through their lands. Because the railroad companies claimed the land where the track was laid, native peoples defended the right to their land.

At the ceremony, a special wooden tie joined the two sections of railway. Two gold spikes, a silver spike, and a gold-and-silver-plated spike were driven into this special tie. This was only for show. The special tie and the spikes were quickly replaced with a regular wooden tie and iron spikes. The final iron spike was driven in by an ordinary worker who had helped build the railroad. The United States was now connected by a railroad.

2 Find Evidence

Look How do the pictures help explain the text?

Reread What was done at a special ceremony to join the section of railway?

3 Make Connections

Talk Look at the people celebrating. Why do you think the railroad officials are celebrating? Why do you think the workers are celebrating? Why would the country be celebrating?

COLLABORATE

Making Inferences

When you read or look at a picture, you often make inferences about the text you read or the picture you see. An **inference** is a decision you make about the meaning of a text or a picture. How do you make an inference?

1. **Read the text carefully all the way through. Look closely at any pictures. Read the captions as you study the pictures.**
   This will help you understand what the text and pictures are about.

2. **Think about what you read and the pictures you studied.**
   An author may not always tell you everything. What questions do you have?

3. **Think about what you already know about this topic.**

4. **Make a decision about the text and pictures.**
   Base your decision on what you know and what you read or see.

 Based on the text you read and the pictures you studied, work with your class to complete the chart below.

Text and Picture Clues and What I Already Know	Inferences
The tie was made of beautiful wood. Two gold spikes, a silver spike, and a gold and silver plated spike were driven into this special tie. I know:	This text means:

Investigate!

Read pages 126–133 in your Research Companion. Use your investigative skills to make inferences about how communities throughout the world are connected to one another. This chart will help you organize your notes.

Text and Picture Clues and What I Already Know	Inferences
There have been huge changes to transportation in the past two hundred years. These changes make it possible for people and goods to travel farther and faster. I know:	This text means:
The photographs that show a telegraph operator and students using a computer. I know:	These photographs mean:
Americans watch foreign movies, too, and they affect how we view other cultures. Many people think of anime or Godzilla movies when they think of Japanese culture. I know:	This text means:

Think About It

Gather Evidence

Review your research. What are some forms of transportation or technologies that connect cultures? How do these connect people within different cultures?

Write About It

Write and Cite Evidence

Write a scene or dialogue about two cultures being connected by technology. How are the cultures connecting? Make inferences about how this connection affects each culture.

_____

_____

_____

_____

_____

_____

_____

_____

_____

_____

_____

Talk About It

Explain

Share your scene or dialogue with a partner.

Connect to the EQ

Economics

Consider

How is your community connected with other communities? What are some products from your local community that are sold to other communities and countries? What products are brought into your community from other communities and countries? How does your community stay unique?

_____

_____

_____

_____

_____

_____

 Inquiry Project Notes

_____

_____

_____

_____

What Makes a Community Unique?

Inquiry Project

Planning a Cultural Event

For this project, you will create a plan for a holiday or festival that celebrates at least three cultures.

Complete Your Project

- ☐ Identify at least three cultures.

- ☐ Conduct research on these cultures.

- ☐ Determine a way to express each of these cultures. Cultures can be expressed through events, dances, art, stories, music, and food.

- ☐ Create a plan for a holiday or festival that celebrates these cultures.

Share Your Project

- ☐ Name the cultures you describe in your plan.

- ☐ Tell about each culture. Explain how each culture helps make your school unique.

- ☐ Share your plan for the holiday or festival. Explain how each culture will be presented.

- ☐ Answer any questions your class might have.

Think about the work you did in this chapter and on your project. Use the questions below to help guide your thoughts.

1. Why did you choose the cultures that you researched?

_____

2. How did you conduct your research? Is there anything you'd do

differently next time? _____

_____

3. How did you make sure that your sources were reliable?_____

_____

Chapter Connections

Use pictures, words, or both to reflect on what you learned in this chapter.

The most interesting thing I learned:

Something I learned from a classmate:

A connection I can make with my own life:

Communities Change Over Time

EQ ESSENTIAL QUESTION

How Does the Past Impact the Present?

In this chapter, you will explore how and why communities grow. You will discover how people have settled and changed their communities. You will also read about what makes these communities special. With a small group, you will work on a chapter project to make a time line describing the development of your community.

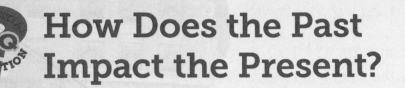

Talk About It COLLABORATE

Talk with a partner about how an event in the past changed your life.

Community Time Line

In this project, you will work with a small group to create a time line showing the sequence of key events that played a role in the development of your community.

Project Checklist

- ☐ **Choose** a community to research. It can be your town, city, country, or state.
- ☐ **Research** the history of the community you chose.
- ☐ **Identify** key events that affected the growth of your community and the places where those events happened.
- ☐ **Write** a description of each event and place. Tell why it helped your community grow.
- ☐ **Find** images to use with each description.
- ☐ **Create** an illustrated time line with your descriptions and images, showing these events in the order they occurred.

My Research Plan

Write down any research questions you have that will help you plan your project. You can add questions as you carry out your research.

_____

_____

_____

_____

Explore Words

Complete this chapter's Word Rater. Write notes as you learn more about each word.

boycott

My Notes

☐ Know It!

_____

☐ Heard It!

_____

☐ Don't Know It!

_____

decade

My Notes

☐ Know It!

_____

☐ Heard It!

_____

☐ Don't Know It!

_____

drought

My Notes

☐ Know It!

_____

☐ Heard It!

_____

☐ Don't Know It!

_____

expedition

My Notes

☐ Know It!

_____

☐ Heard It!

_____

☐ Don't Know It!

_____

innovation

My Notes

☐ Know It!

_____

☐ Heard It!

_____

☐ Don't Know It!

_____

monument

- ☐ Know It!
- ☐ Heard It!
- ☐ Don't Know It!

My Notes

_____

_____

_____

peninsula

- ☐ Know It!
- ☐ Heard It!
- ☐ Don't Know It!

My Notes

_____

_____

_____

public services

- ☐ Know It!
- ☐ Heard It!
- ☐ Don't Know It!

My Notes

_____

_____

_____

strait

- ☐ Know It!
- ☐ Heard It!
- ☐ Don't Know It!

My Notes

_____

_____

_____

taxes

- ☐ Know It!
- ☐ Heard It!
- ☐ Don't Know It!

My Notes

_____

_____

_____

Lesson 1

How Did Conflict and Cooperation Shape Early Communities?

Lesson Outcomes

What Am I Learning?

In this lesson, you will use your investigative skills to find out how European settlers lived with Native Americans.

Why Am I Learning It?

Reading and talking about how the Americas were settled will help you understand how conflict and cooperation shape communities over time.

How Will I Know That I Learned It?

You will be able to tell about changes that happen when different cultures meet.

Talk About It

COLLABORATE

Look closely at the picture. Who are the people? What are they doing? What do you think they see?

Explorers in North America

A Clash of Cultures

Read the first paragraph. What do you think this text will be about?

Read the article. Circle words you do not know.

Underline what the American settlers and government expected of the Native Americans.

Discuss with a partner how Native Americans changed because of American settlers.

My Notes

_____

_____

_____

_____

_____

_____

Native Americans were the first people to live in what is now the United States. They had lived in the area for thousands of years. They had their own beliefs and ways of life. European settlers who came to North America brought their own cultures with them. Often, these cultures and ways of life were very different from how Native Americans lived.

Many settlers felt their cultures were the only way of life. They thought it would help the Native Americans to live as they did. They expected them to speak and dress like they did. They expected them to change their religions and give up their ways of life. Native Americans lost much of their culture during this time.

Native Americans had their own cultures and ways of life.

Potawatomi people gathered for a special occasion in 1906.

In the 1800s, many states were added to the United States—from Ohio to California. American settlers moved into those regions. They took the best land for themselves. They made the Native Americans move from their homelands. The United States government made the Native Americans live on small reservations.

One of these Native American groups was the Potawatomi. They lived in what is now Michigan, Indiana, and Illinois. When European settlers started arriving in the area, the Potawatomi moved west to Wisconsin. The government made treaties, or agreements, for the Native Americans to give up their land in return for payments. The Treaties of Fort Wayne in 1803 and 1809 particularly affected the Potawatomi. They were pushed to Kansas and then Oklahoma. As the Potawatomi moved west, they adapted to their new homeland. They learned from other Plains groups how to hunt bison.

Copyright © McGraw-Hill Education
PHOTO: Library of Congress Prints and Photographs Division [LC-USZ62-132033]

2 Find Evidence

Reread How did the American settlers and government treat the Native Americans? What information from the text supports your ideas?

Look at the photographs. How do they help you understand how the lives of Native Americans changed?

3 Make Connections

Talk Why do you think settlers thought their cultures were the only way of life? Discuss your answer with a partner.

COLLABORATE

Connect to Now Do Native Americans live in your community today?

Explore Chronology

Identifying the **chronology**, or the order in which events occur, will help you understand how events in history are connected.

1. **Read the text once all the way through.**
   This will help you understand what the text is about.

2. **Look at the section titles to see how the text is organized.**
   Titles may offer clues as to which important events are discussed.

3. **Watch for specific dates.**
   Are the events presented in chronological order? It may help to look for sentences that begin with a date. Note that dates could be specific, such as "In 1529." They could also express a range of time, such as "In the 1800s."

4. **Find key facts about the events.**
   While reading, ask yourself what key facts are most important to remember about the conflict and cooperation between the Europeans and Americans and the Native Americans.

Based on the text you read, work with your class to complete the chart below.

Time Period	Key Facts
1800s	

Investigate!

Read pages 144–153 in your Research Companion. Use your investigative skills to look for text evidence that tells you when and what happened. This chart will help you organize your notes.

Time Period	Key Facts
1500s	
1600s	
1700s	
1800s	

Think About It

Gather Evidence

Review your research. Based on the information you have gathered, how did the lives of Native Americans change with the arrival of newcomers?

Write About It

Write and Cite Evidence

In your opinion, what are some positive things that happen when different cultures meet? What are some negative things?

_____

_____

_____

_____

_____

_____

_____

_____

_____

_____

_____

Talk About It

Defend Your Claim

Take turns discussing your responses with a classmate. Do you think the meeting of cultures in the early years of the United States was more positive or negative?

History

Connect to the

Pull It Together

Think about the people and events you read and talked about in this lesson. How did they change things for the United States today?

_____

_____

_____

_____

Inquiry Project Notes

_____

_____

_____

_____

_____

What Makes a Community Grow?

Lesson Outcomes

What Am I Learning?

In this lesson, you will use your investigative skills to find out what makes a community grow.

Why Am I Learning It?

Reading and talking about the growth of communities will help you understand the reasons why communities grow and change.

How Will I Know That I Learned It?

You will be able to write a paragraph explaining the main reason people move to a new place.

Talk About It

COLLABORATE

Look at the photograph on the next page. What words would you use to describe the buildings in the photo?

A lumbering camp in Michigan during the late 1800s

Moving into Michigan

1 Inspect

Look at the graph. What does it show?

Circle the year when Michigan's population was almost 3 million.

Place a box around the following:

- the point on the graph showing the population in 1920
- the point on the graph showing the population in 1950

My Notes

_____

_____

_____

_____

_____

_____

_____

_____

_____

Why did Michigan's population more than double between 1900 and 1950? The most important reason is the car industry.

During the late 1800s, Michigan had a successful lumber industry. In order to move the large logs, workers needed strong wagons pulled by horses. There were many companies in Michigan that built wagons. In the early 1900s, demand began for a new type of vehicle: the car. Michigan's wagon companies were ready to build them.

By 1940, more than half of the world's cars were built in Detroit, Michigan. Almost every car company had a factory there. People came from all over the country to find work in the automobile industry. As the population grew, there were needs for other kinds of jobs, too. For example, a growing city needs teachers, firefighters, grocers, and carpenters.

Another reason Michigan's population increased was the Great Migration. During the first half of the 1900s, millions of African Americans left the South. They moved to get away from segregation, the practice of keeping people of different races separate. They also hoped to find better jobs. Many people came to Detroit for work. Between 1910 and 1920, Detroit's African American population grew six times greater.

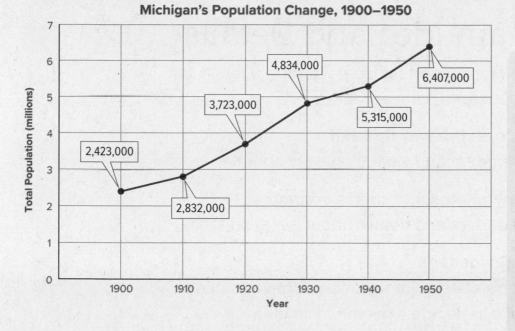

Michigan's Population Change, 1900–1950

2,423,000

2,832,000

3,723,000

4,834,000

5,315,000

6,407,000

Total Population (millions)

Year

How to Read a Line Graph

To read a line graph, look at the graph's title and the labels. These tell you what the graph is about. The points, or dots, on the line show the information for each year. Trace the line connecting the points to see changes over time. On this graph, the line goes up. This means the population has grown. Some parts of the line are steeper than the others. When the line is steeper, it shows that the change in population was greater.

2 Find Evidence

Reread Look at the points for 1900 and 1950. What happened to Michigan's population during this time? Did more people live in Michigan in 1940 than in 1910? How do you know?

3 Make Connections

Talk Discuss with a partner how the graph supports the main idea of the article.

Explore Main Idea and Details

The **main idea** is the most important idea of a topic. Details tell more about the main idea.

1. **Read the text once all the way through.**
   This will help you understand what the text is about.

2. **Look closely at any photos and charts or graphs.**
   This will help you understand details about the main idea.

3. **Decide on the main idea.**
   It may or may not be stated. Sometimes you have to think about all the details to decide what the main idea is.

4. **Look for details that tell more about the main idea.**
   The details will help you better understand the main idea.

COLLABORATE

Based on the text you read, work with your class to complete the web below.

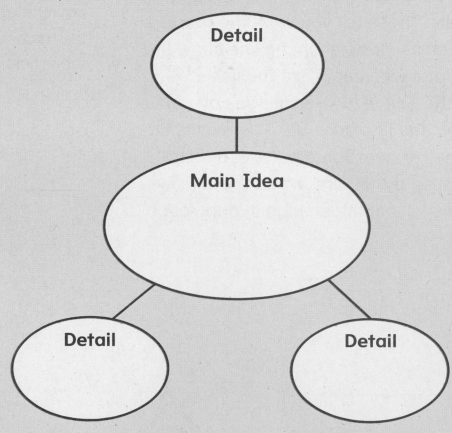

Detail

Main Idea

Detail

Detail

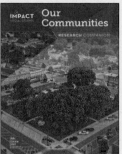

Investigate!

Read pages 154–161 in your Research Companion. Use your investigative skills to look for details that support the main idea. This web will help you organize your notes.

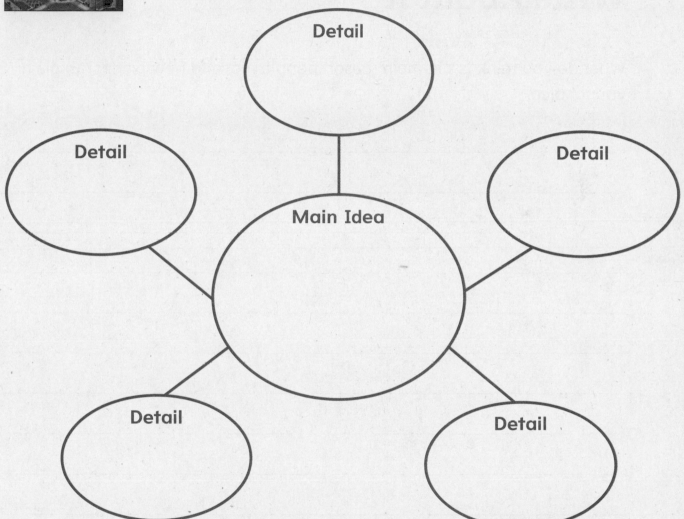

Detail

Detail

Detail

Main Idea

Detail

Detail

Think About It

Gather Evidence

Based on your research, why do you think people migrate to a new place?

Write About It

Write and Cite Evidence

What do you think is the main reason people move to new places? Explain your choice.

_____

_____

_____

_____

_____

_____

_____

_____

_____

_____

_____

_____

Talk About It

Explain

Compare your choice with the choice of a classmate. Take turns explaining your choices. Discuss why people often have several reasons for moving.

Geography

Connect to the

Pull It Together

What are some ways that a community has changed over the years? What causes communities to change over time? How does that impact the present?

_____

_____

_____

_____

Inquiry Project Notes

_____

_____

_____

_____

_____

_____

Lesson Outcomes

What Am I Learning?

In this lesson, you will use your investigative skills to find out how a community changes over time.

Why Am I Learning It?

Reading and talking about what life was like in the past will help you learn how a community can change.

How Will I Know That I Learned It?

You will be able to write a paragraph about life in the past and explain how life is different today. You also will be able to give reasons why communities change.

The St. Louis Cathedral in New Orleans, Louisiana

Talk About It

COLLABORATE

Look closely at the pictures. Describe the buildings. Do they look like the buildings you see in your community today? Do they seem old or modern?

Faneuil Hall in Boston, Massachusetts

1 Inspect

Read the title. What do you think this text will be about?

Highlight the names of two cities that show the places from which the early settlers came.

Underline the words that describe things in the different cultures that make up the United States.

Discuss with a partner what you think your community was like in the past.

My Notes

_____

_____

_____

_____

_____

_____

_____

How the Past Can Be Seen Today

Read the names of these Florida cities: Boca Raton and Punta Gorda. The names are Spanish. This is because the Spanish formed these communities. The names help you understand the history of these cities. You can also learn about a community's history by looking at its buildings. The way a building looks can tell you who built it and when it was built. Buildings with red clay tile roofs and thick white walls are built in a Spanish style.

The population of the United States is diverse. Each community is made up of people from many different ethnic groups and backgrounds. Native Americans have lived in the United States for thousands of years. Other groups of people came more recently. The British settlers named many of the cities and states in New England after places in England. French settlers named New Orleans, Louisiana, after a city in France. German settlers named Fredericksburg, Texas, after a city in Germany. Today, people from all over the world make the United States home.

People from many ethnic groups have affected your community. The signs you see or even the house you live in can show your community's history. You may eat foods from different cultures. You may celebrate the holidays of other cultures. The people who lived in your community in the past helped make your community what it is like today.

Foods from many different cultures are available in the United States.

2 Find Evidence

Reread What features of a community today tell you about the cultures and people of its past?

Underline examples in the text of ethnic groups.

3 Make Connections

Talk Is there a part of your community named for something in the past? Why do you think it is important for a community to do things to show its history?

Explore Compare and Contrast

To **compare** is to tell how things are alike. To **contrast** is to tell how things are different. Your social studies text will sometimes compare and contrast two things or two time periods.

1. **Read the text once all the way through.**
   This will help you understand what the text is about.

2. **Look for words that signal a comparison or a contrast.**
   The text may use words such as *like, the same,* and *both* to compare two things. It may use words such as *unlike* and *different* to contrast two things.

3. **Now look for the big ideas that are being compared.**
   A text may compare and contrast two groups of people, two forms of transportation, or two time periods. Look for key words such as *in the past* and *in the present*.

4. **Ask: *How are these the same? How are they different?***
   Make a list or take notes on what is being compared.

 Based on the text you read, work with your class to complete the Venn diagram below.

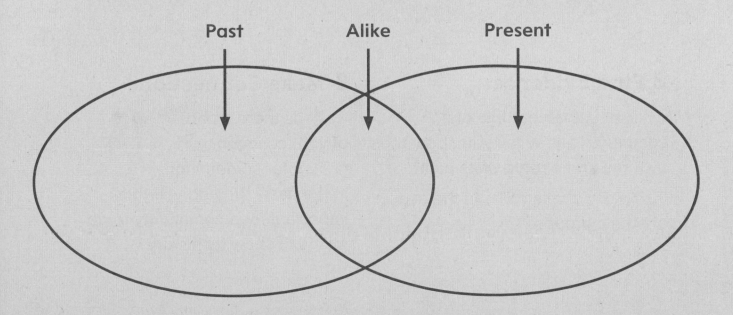

Past   Alike   Present

Investigate!

Read pages 162–171 in your Research Companion. Use your investigative skills to look for text evidence that tells you how things in the past and today are alike and different. This chart will help you organize your notes.

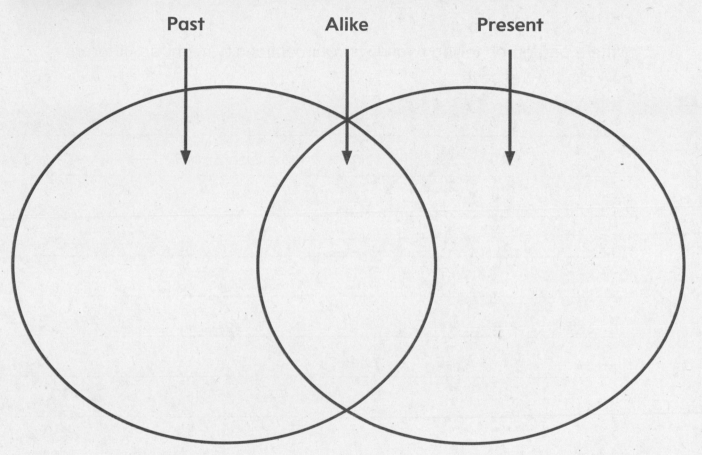

Past   Alike   Present

Think About It

Gather Evidence

What causes communities to change over time?

Write About It

Write and Cite Evidence

Write a paragraph telling two ways your community might be different now than in the past.

_____

_____

_____

_____

_____

_____

_____

_____

_____

_____

_____

_____

Talk About It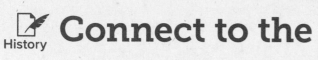

Share Your Ideas

Read your paragraph to a partner. Then talk about how your community today is different from a century ago.

History

Connect to the

Pull It Together

Think about the changes you have read and talked about in this lesson. Which change do you think had the biggest impact on your community?

_____

_____

_____

_____

_____

Inquiry Project Notes

_____

_____

_____

_____

_____

_____

Lesson Outcomes

What Am I Learning?

In this lesson, you will use your investigative skills to explore ways in which people and events change communities.

Why Am I Learning It?

Reading and talking about ways in which people and events have changed communities can help you understand your community better.

How Will I Know That I Learned It?

You will be able to write a letter to one of the people you have learned about in this lesson to explain how he or she has changed your community.

Talk About It

COLLABORATE

Look closely at the photos. What are some changes about the different devices that you notice?

The cell phone has changed a lot since early cell phones.

Making Communication Mobile

1 Inspect

Read the title and the Primary Source. What do you think this text will be about?

Circle words you do not know.

Underline clues that will help you answer:

- Who is Martin Cooper?
- How did he change the way people live and do business?
- Why were New Yorkers surprised to see what Martin Cooper was doing?

My Notes

_____

_____

_____

_____

_____

_____

_____

PRIMARY SOURCE

In Their Words... Martin Cooper

"As I walked down the street while talking on the phone . . . New Yorkers gaped at the sight of someone actually moving around while making a phone call."

— Martin Cooper, 2011

Martin Cooper, inventor of the first truly mobile phone

To make a telephone call in the mid-twentieth century, you had to go where the phone was: in your home, in the school office, or in a phone booth. Phones were connected to the phone system by a telephone wire. If you moved to another city, you needed to get a new phone number.

Martin Cooper changed this forever. He and a team of engineers designed the first mobile phone a person could carry anywhere. Cooper made the first cell phone call in 1973. However, it took ten years before people could actually buy a cell phone.

The early mobile phones were big and heavy, but technology has improved them. Today's smartphone fits into a pocket. It can do many things. It is a camera, calendar, calculator, and notepad. You can text, e-mail, play games, or surf the web on your phone.

The graph below shows the number of people who owned cell phones over a period of thirty years.

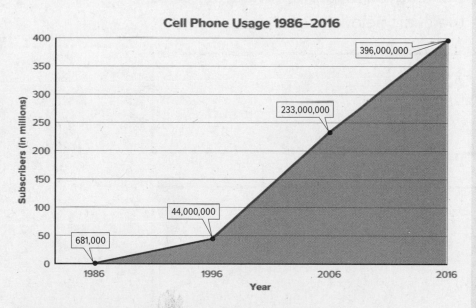

Cell Phone Usage 1986–2016

396,000,000

233,000,000

44,000,000

681,000

Subscribers (in millions)

Year

This graph shows how the number of cell phones has increased over a thirty-year period.

2 Find Evidence

Interpret the Graph Draw a straight line on the graph from the dot at 1986 to the dot at 2016. What do you notice about the line between 1986 and 2016?

Underline the dates and events in the text above.

Write the dates in the correct place on the graph.

Talk What are some possible reasons cell phone use changed so much between 1986 and 1996?

3 Make Connections

Talk How has the increased availability of cell phones solved problems? How has it created new problems?

COLLABORATE

Explore Problem and Solution

A **problem** is a situation that, if solved, will improve. A **solution** is a way to solve a problem.

1. **Read the text all the way through.**
    This will help you to identify problems that are being described.

2. **Find any steps that show how the problem might be solved.**
    Look for details that explain what was done to help solve the problem.

3. **Find any solutions that are provided.**
    Look for ways that the problem was solved.

 Based on the text you read, work with your class to complete the chart below.

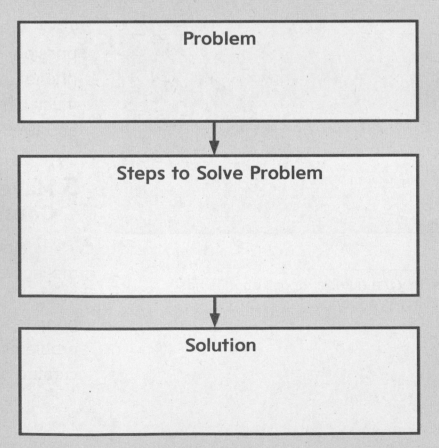

Investigate!

Read pages 172–179 in your Research Companion. Use your investigative skills to look for text evidence that tells you the problems people and communities faced and the solutions to these problems. This chart will help you organize your notes.

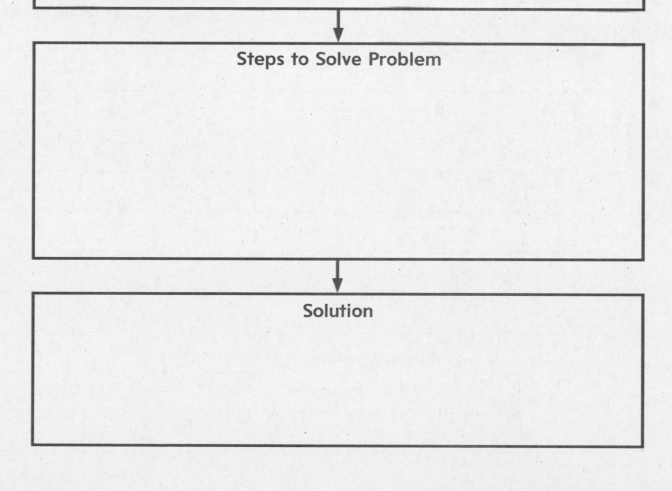

Problem

African Americans were enslaved and treated unequally.

Thomas Edison and Helen Keller had to find ways to overcome disabilities.

Laws treated African Americans unequally.

Natural disasters cause destruction.

Steps to Solve Problem

Solution

Think About It

Gather Evidence

Review your research. Based on the information you have gathered, describe at least two problems people have faced. What were their solutions to these problems?

Write About It

Write and Cite Evidence

Write a letter to one of the people you have learned about in this lesson. Tell this person how he or she has impacted your community.

_____

_____

_____

_____

_____

_____

_____

_____

_____

_____

Talk About It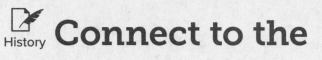

Explain
Share your letter with a partner. Discuss why each of you wrote to the person you chose.

Connect to the

Pull It Together
What people and events have changed your community? List three ideas to share with others.

1. _____

2. _____

3. _____

   _____

Inquiry Project Notes

_____

_____

_____

_____

_____

_____

What Can Comparing Different Communities Tell Us About How Communities Change Over Time?

Lesson Outcomes

What Am I Learning?

In this lesson, you will use your investigative skills to find out how communities change over time.

Why Am I Learning It?

Reading and talking about how communities change will help you understand how your community has become what it is today.

How Will I Know That I Learned It?

You will be able to create a list of topics you want to research about your own community.

Talk About It

COLLABORATE

Look closely at the photos on the next page. What do you see? What can we learn about the past from these?

This Detroit museum shows the impact the automobile had on the development of the city.

Large murals span two outside walls of the National Museum in Malaysia's capital city, Kuala Lumpur. They show economic activities, cultural traditions, and events from the country's history.

1 Inspect

Read the title and look at the chart. What do you think you will learn?

Underline clues that will help you answer:

- What is a time line?
- In what order does it list events?

Circle the events that happened first on each side of the time line.

Draw a box around the events that happened most recently on each side of the time line.

Read the dates and the events on the time line.

- What happened in 1998 in Kuala Lumpur?
- What year did Detroit become Michigan's capital?

My Notes

_____

_____

_____

Charting History on Time Lines

If you want to tell people what you did today, you would most likely list events in a certain order. You would tell what you did first, or earliest, in the day. Then you would describe later activities. You would end by explaining what you did most recently.

In history, we do the same thing with time lines. A time line lists historical events in the order in which they occurred. Events are listed from first, or those in the most distant past, to last, or those in the most recent past. The past refers to events that happened before now.

A time line most often lists information from left to right or from top to bottom. Study this example.

The steps at Batu caves in Kuala Lumpur

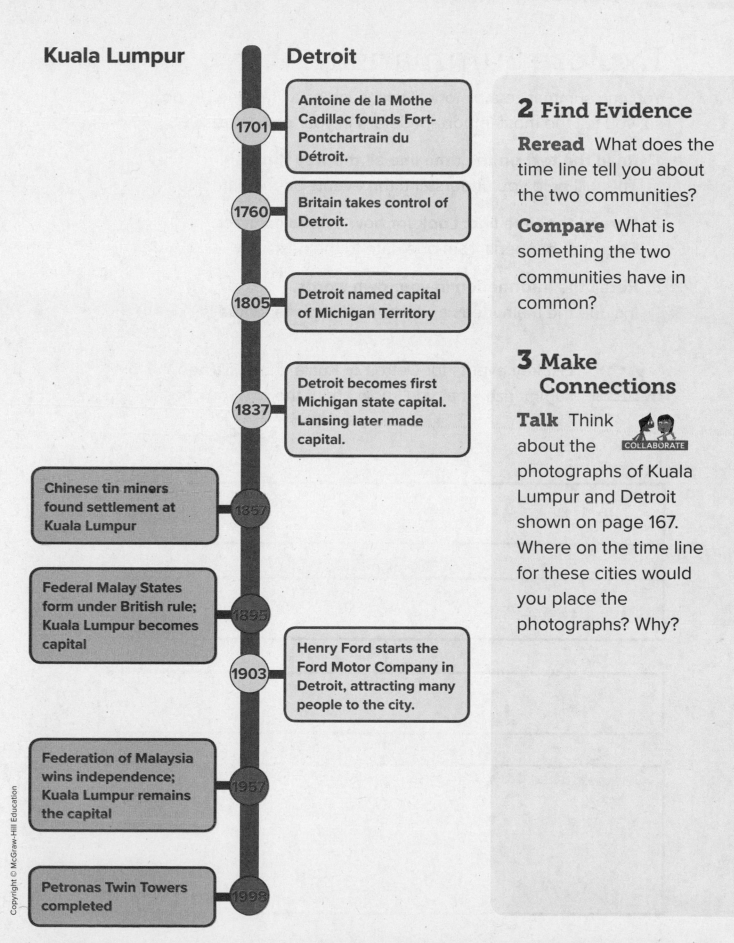

Kuala Lumpur

Detroit

1701 Antoine de la Mothe Cadillac founds Fort-Pontchartrain du Détroit.

1760 Britain takes control of Detroit.

1805 Detroit named capital of Michigan Territory

1837 Detroit becomes first Michigan state capital. Lansing later made capital.

1857 Chinese tin miners found settlement at Kuala Lumpur

1895 Federal Malay States form under British rule; Kuala Lumpur becomes capital

1903 Henry Ford starts the Ford Motor Company in Detroit, attracting many people to the city.

1957 Federation of Malaysia wins independence; Kuala Lumpur remains the capital

1998 Petronas Twin Towers completed

2 Find Evidence

Reread What does the time line tell you about the two communities?

Compare What is something the two communities have in common?

3 Make Connections

Talk Think about the photographs of Kuala Lumpur and Detroit shown on page 167. Where on the time line for these cities would you place the photographs? Why?

COLLABORATE

Explore Summarizing

You can summarize a historical text, such as a time line. To do so, you tell the most important details in your own words.

1. **Read the text on the time line all the way through.**
   This will help you understand the events on the time line.

2. **Reread the time line. Look for how events connect.**
   See what happens from one date to the next.

3. **Retell the information in your own words.**
   Include the main ideas and the most important details.

List key events for Detroit or Kuala Lumpur. Then summarize what you know about the city you chose.

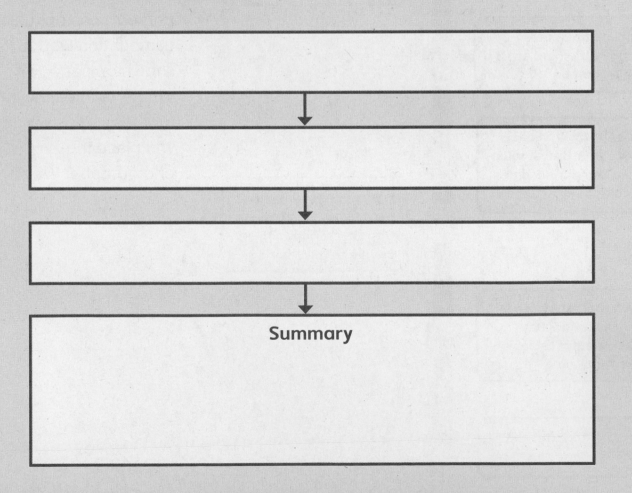

Summary

Investigate!

Read pages 180–187 in your Research Companion. Use your investigative skills to look for text evidence that tells you more about how the communities of Kuala Lumpur and Detroit developed and changed over time. The charts will help you organize your information for each community.

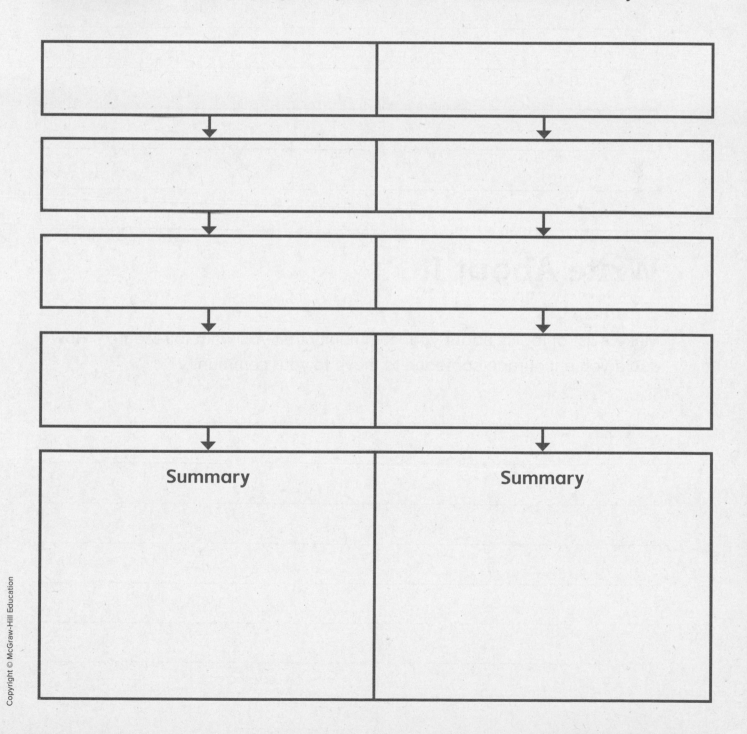

↓ ↓

↓ ↓

↓ ↓

↓ ↓

Summary	**Summary**

Think About It

Gather Evidence

Based on your research about Kuala Lumpur and Detroit, what information do you want to find out about your community? What resources could you use to learn about your community and its history?

_____

_____

_____

_____

_____

Write About It

Explain

Make a list of topics about your community that you want to research. How could you encourage someone to move to your community?

_____

_____

_____

_____

_____

_____

Talk About It

Explain

Compare lists with a partner. Pick features from both lists that you think would encourage people to move to your community.

Geography

Connect to the

Pull It Together

Think about ways that your community has changed over the years. How have these changes affected the lives of people living in the community today?

_____

_____

_____

_____

_____

_____

_____

Inquiry Project Notes

_____

_____

_____

Lesson 6

What Makes My Community Special?

Lesson Outcomes

What Am I Learning?

In this lesson, you will use your investigative skills to find out how communities are special.

Why Am I Learning It?

Reading and talking about why a community is special will help you learn how geography, history, and cultures affect the people who live in a community.

How Will I Know That I Learned It?

You will be able to tell what makes a community special. You will be able to write about your own community and describe what makes it special.

Talk About It

COLLABORATE

Look closely at the photo on the next page. What details in it do you find interesting? What do you think it shows about the community?

Native American dancers perform a traditional dance.

Linking to the Past

1 Inspect

Read the title. What do you think this text will be about?

- **Circle** any words you do not know.
- **Underline** details that explain why streetcars are important to New Orleans.

My Notes

_____

_____

_____

_____

_____

_____

_____

_____

_____

_____

New Orleans became known for streetcars, jazz clubs, and Mardi Gras during the 1900s. Tourists from around the world visited the city. Levees and canals were built to protect the city from flooding. Then Hurricane Katrina struck the city in 2005. The levees were no match for the storm. Much of New Orleans flooded. It took many years for New Orleans to rebuild again. New Orleans has kept links to its rich and interesting past. Let's look at one of those links.

New Orleans's streetcars are famous around the world. They are one of the oldest street railways still in operation. New Orleans was the first place west of the Allegheny Mountains to have a street railway service. Streetcars first began in 1835 to connect New Orleans and a suburb. They were powered by steam.

Much of New Orleans was rebuilt after Hurricane Katrina.

Streetcars are a symbol of New Orleans. Even today, they run on many New Orleans streets.

Steam trains were replaced by horse-drawn cars and then by electricity in 1893. New Orleans had more than 350 streetcars, that each held twenty-eight people, by the beginning of the 1900s. Some streetcars were painted olive green while others were painted red and gold.

During the 1930s, people preferred cars and buses. Fewer streetcars were needed. By the 1960s, most streetcars were retired. One streetcar line became a National Historic Landmark.

In 1988, New Orleans built a new streetcar line. Some people used the streetcars to get to work. Tourists found the streetcars charming and a great way to see some of New Orleans's historic sites. More and more people began using streetcars again. Today, streetcars are an important part of New Orleans transportation and history.

2 Find Evidence

Reread Why have streetcars in New Orleans once again become a popular form of transportation?

Underline clues that support your ideas.

3 Make Connections

Talk Discuss with a partner COLLABORATE why streetcars are an important part of New Orleans's history. What do you know about your community's history? What things from the past do you still find where you live?

Explore Drawing Conclusions

A **conclusion** is a decision you make about a topic. You use what you already know and information from what you are reading to draw a conclusion.

1. **Read the text.**
   Think about how the details and ideas in the text are connected.

2. **Think about what you already know about this topic.**
   Sometimes the author does not tell you everything. You have to use what you already know to understand the text.

3. **Draw a conclusion.**
   Draw a conclusion using what you read and what you know.

Based on the text you read, work with your class to complete the chart below to answer the question: "How do the people of New Orleans feel about the streetcars?"

Text Clues and What I Already Know	Conclusion

Investigate!

Read pages 188–195 in your Research Companion. Use your investigative skills to look for text evidence that tells you why communities are special. Then draw conclusions about what makes a community a special place. This chart will help you organize your notes.

Text Clues and What I Already Know About Communities	Conclusions

Think About It

Review

Recall what you have learned through your research.
Why do you think all communities are different?

Write About It

Define

What things can make a community special?

_____

_____

_____

_____

_____

_____

In Your Opinion

Write a blog post about your community, its people,
and its places. List reasons why you think your community
is special.

_____

_____

_____

_____

_____

_____

Talk About It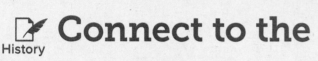

Compare and Contrast

Share your blog with a partner. Compare and contrast your ideas.
Then brainstorm additional reasons why your community is special.

History

Connect to the

Pull It Together

Think about the role history has played in your community. How have events
and people of the past helped make your community special?

_____

_____

_____

_____

Inquiry Project Notes

_____

_____

_____

_____

_____

How Does the Past Impact the Present?

Inquiry Project

Community Time Line

For this project, you'll research past events that have made an impact in the development of your community.

Complete Your Project

☐ Research the history of your community.

☐ Identify key events that affected the growth of your community and the places where those events happened.

☐ Using words and pictures, describe each event.

☐ Assemble your time line by arranging the events in the order that they happened.

Share Your Project

☐ Show your time line to the class. Imagine that you are helping visitors get to know your community.

☐ Explain how your team chose which events and locations to include in the time line.

☐ Have each team member tell about part of the time line.

☐ Answer any questions your class might have.

Think about the work you did in this chapter and on your project. Use the questions below to help guide your thoughts.

1. How did you decide on which events to include in your time line?

_____

2. How did you conduct your research? Is there anything you'd do differently next time? _____

_____

3. How did you make sure that your sources were reliable? _____

_____

Chapter Connections

Use pictures, words, or both to reflect on what you learned in this chapter.

The most interesting thing I learned:

Something I learned from a classmate:

A connection I can make with my own life:

Step Back in Time

CHARACTERS

Narrator	**Teacher**
Tour Guide	**Maria** *a girl from 1910*
Maya *a girl from the present day*	**Maria's little sisters and brothers** *(non-speaking parts)*
Binh *a boy from the present day*	**Joe** *Maria's brother*

Narrator: Maya and Binh are in the third grade. They are on a class trip. They are visiting a museum to learn about immigrants who came to their community long ago. To their surprise, they find an unexpected exhibit.

Tour Guide: Welcome to the museum. Today we will learn what life was like for people who came to the United States long ago. Let's start by seeing the kind of place where many immigrants lived.

(Maya, Binh, and the Teacher follow the Tour Guide.)

Tour Guide: More than one hundred years ago, an immigrant family lived in an apartment like this. Ten people might have slept in this one room.

Maya: And I thought my apartment was crowded!

Tour Guide: Please follow me to the next room.

(The Tour Guide leaves. The Teacher follows. Maya turns to leave, but Binh stops her.)

Binh: Look, Maya. A door! Let's take a look.

Narrator: This was no ordinary door. This door belonged to a time machine.

(Binh opens the door, and Maya follows him. Maria, a 10-year-old girl from 1910, is cooking over a stove. Smaller children surround her.)

Maria: Hello. Are you here to rent the apartment upstairs?

Maya: I don't think so.

Maria: Then why are you here?

Binh: We're here on a school trip.

Maria: School? Don't you have to work?

Maya: No. We're only eight.

Maria: Well, I'm 10. I've had a job since I was five.

Binh: What kind of work do you do?

Maria: I help my mother make clothes. She sells them. *(Pause)* What strange clothes you are wearing. We do not wear such things in 1910.

Maya: *(to Binh)* Did she say 1910? What does she mean?

Binh: *(to Maya)* We must have traveled back in time!

Maria: Where are you from?

Binh: I was born in Vietnam.

Maya: I'm from California.

Maria: I was born in Italy. It's hard moving to a new country, isn't it? Do you miss your homeland?

Binh: Yes, I miss my grandparents. They still live in Vietnam.

Maria: I miss my grandparents, too! I visited them every day when I lived in Italy.

Binh: I did, too, in Vietnam.

Maria: Now, I'll never see them again.

Maya: Can't you take an airplane and fly back to see them?

Maria: Airplane? Fly? What are you talking about? I'd have to take a boat to go back to Italy. Besides, it costs too much money.

Binh: Do you like it in the United States?

Maria: Yes, I like a lot of things about the United States. People come here from all over the world.

Maya: I like that about the United States, too.

Maria: But it was hard to learn to speak English. My brother Joe taught me. He goes to school during the day. He works at night lighting the street lamps. Oh, I hear him walking up the stairs now.

(Joe enters. He carries books under his arm.)

Joe: Hello, Maria. Who are these people?

Maria: Joe, these are my new friends. *(to Binh)* Don't worry about missing your homeland. Life will get better, I promise.

(Maria and Joe say "goodbye" as Binh and Maya exit through the door.)

Maya: Wow! Life was very different in 1910!

Binh: Can you imagine going to school and working?

(The Teacher walks in.)

Teacher: *(smiling)* There you are! I hope you saw something interesting.

Binh/Maya: *(speaking together)* We sure did!

Talk About It

COLLABORATE

With a partner, discuss what your first day at school might be like if you moved to a different country.

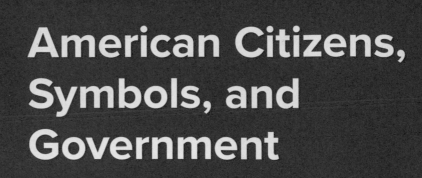

Chapter 5

American Citizens, Symbols, and Government

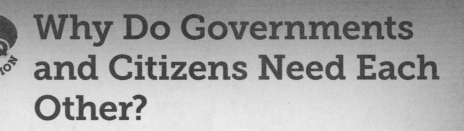

Why Do Governments and Citizens Need Each Other?

In this chapter, you will learn how our governments are organized and how they work. You will learn about citizenship. You will also explore what it means to be a good citizen. With your class, you will work on a chapter project to write a constitution that sets classroom rules.

Talk About It COLLABORATE

Talk with your partner about questions you have about governments and being a good citizen.

Creating a Classroom Constitution

In this project, you will work with your class to create a classroom constitution that sets the rules everyone must follow to make your classroom a fair and safe community.

Project Checklist

☐ **Set** a purpose for your classroom constitution.

☐ **Think** about how you should behave in the classroom.

☐ **List** a set of rules that everyone must follow.

☐ **Discuss** the consequences for breaking a rule.

☐ **Write** a constitution that describes rules for your class and the consequences for breaking a rule.

☐ **Agree** to follow the constitution.

My Research Plan

Write down any research questions you have that will help you plan your project. You can add questions as you carry out your research.

_____

_____

_____

_____

_____

_____

Complete this chapter's Word Rater. Write notes as you learn more about each word.

compromise
- ☐ Know It!
- ☐ Heard It!
- ☐ Don't Know It!

My Notes
_____
_____
_____

executive branch
- ☐ Know It!
- ☐ Heard It!
- ☐ Don't Know It!

My Notes
_____
_____
_____

federal
- ☐ Know It!
- ☐ Heard It!
- ☐ Don't Know It!

My Notes
_____
_____
_____

hero
- ☐ Know It!
- ☐ Heard It!
- ☐ Don't Know It!

My Notes
_____
_____
_____

judicial branch
- ☐ Know It!
- ☐ Heard It!
- ☐ Don't Know It!

My Notes
_____
_____
_____

jury

☐ Know It!
☐ Heard It!
☐ Don't Know It!

My Notes

_____

_____

_____

justice

☐ Know It!
☐ Heard It!
☐ Don't Know It!

My Notes

_____

_____

_____

legislative branch

☐ Know It!
☐ Heard It!
☐ Don't Know It!

My Notes

_____

_____

_____

rights

☐ Know It!
☐ Heard It!
☐ Don't Know It!

My Notes

_____

_____

_____

volunteer

☐ Know It!
☐ Heard It!
☐ Don't Know It!

My Notes

_____

_____

_____

What Makes Democracy Work?

Lesson Outcomes

What Am I Learning?

In this lesson, you will use your investigative skills to find out about the United States Constitution.

Why Am I Learning It?

Reading and talking about the Constitution will help you understand how our government is set up.

How Will I Know That I Learned It?

You will be able to write a list of items that might be in a classroom constitution.

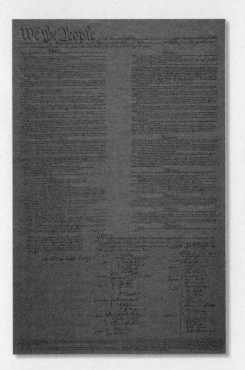

The U.S. Constitution

Talk About It

COLLABORATE

Look closely at the picture on the next page. What do you think the room was used for? What clues in the picture help you know this?

The Assembly Room in Independence Hall, Philadelphia, Pennsylvania

Preamble of the United States Constitution

1 Inspect

Read the first paragraph. What is the preamble?

- **Circle** any words in the preamble that you do not know.
- **Underline** the words that tell *who* the Constitution is written for.
- **Discuss** with a partner the reasons *why* the Constitution was written. Then restate one of the reasons in your own words.

My Notes

_____

_____

_____

_____

_____

_____

_____

_____

Have you ever heard or seen the words "We the People"? You can find them at the beginning of our nation's Constitution. This part is called the preamble. The preamble introduces the Constitution. The opening words show that the United States government is run by its people and for its people. The preamble also lists the reasons why the Constitution was written. Let's read the preamble to find out more!

PRIMARY SOURCE

"We the People of the United States, in Order to form a more perfect Union, establish Justice, insure domestic Tranquility, provide for the common defence, promote the general Welfare, and secure the Blessings of Liberty to ourselves and our Posterity, do ordain and establish this Constitution for the United States of America."

—Preamble to the United States Constitution

The United States Constitution begins with the words "We the People."

The preamble also tells about American beliefs. For example, the people of the United States are very important. The government gets its power from the people. Also, it is important for the states to join together. They are stronger as one country.

2 Find Evidence

Reread the preamble. How many reasons are listed for why the Constitution was written? Why do you think the founders listed so many reasons?

Think about the phrase "promote the general Welfare." What does the word *welfare* mean? Name a word that has a similar meaning.

3 Make Connections

Talk Discuss with a partner the reasons why the Constitution was written. Which do you think is most important? Why?

Explore Main Idea and Details

The topic is what a text is about. The **main idea** is the most important idea of a topic. **Details** tell more about the main idea.

1. **Read the text once all the way through.**
   This will help you understand what the text is about.

2. **Use section titles to identify topics.**
   A section title often tells you the topic of that section.

3. **Ask yourself:** *What is the most important idea about this topic?*
   The most important idea is the main idea of the text.

4. **Look for information that tells more about the main idea.**
   These are details. They help you understand the main idea.

COLLABORATE
Based on the text you read, work with your class to complete the chart below.

Main Idea	Details
The preamble introduces the United States Constitution.	

Investigate!

Read pages 206–215 in your Research Companion. Use your investigative skills to look for details that tell more about the main ideas listed in the chart. This chart will help you organize your notes.

Main Ideas	Details
The Articles of Confederation was the first plan for the government of the United States.	
At the Constitutional Convention, a new constitution was written for the United States.	
Democracy is an important part of American government.	
Other countries have governments that are similar to or different from ours.	

Think About It

Take a Stand

Why might a constitution for your classroom be helpful?
Think about what might be contained in the constitution.

Write About It

Write a List of Ideas

Work with a partner to write a list of items that might be in
a classroom constitution.

_____

_____

_____

_____

_____

_____

_____

_____

_____

_____

_____

Talk About It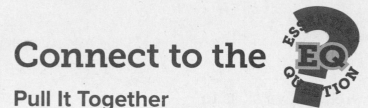

Compare and Contrast

Share your list with your classmates. Compare and contrast your ideas.
Then discuss which ideas are most important to include in a class constitution.

Civics

Connect to the EQ

Pull It Together

How does the Constitution help our government and its citizens
to work together?

_____

_____

_____

_____

 Inquiry Project Notes

_____

_____

_____

_____

_____

_____

Lesson Outcomes

What Am I Learning?

In this lesson, you will use your investigative skills to understand the branches of government.

Why Am I Learning It?

Reading and talking about how the government is set up will help you understand how the government works.

How Will I Know That I Learned It?

You will be able to support an opinion about which branch of government you think is most important.

In Their Words... Theodore Roosevelt

"We get in the habit of speaking of the Government as if it were something apart from us. Now, the Government is us—we are the Government, you and I. And the Government is going to do well or ill accordingly as we make up our minds that the affairs of the Government shall be managed."

—Speech by President Theodore Roosevelt given in Asheville, North Carolina, 1902, as recorded by Robert C. V. Meyers

Copyright © McGraw-Hill Education
PHOTO: Library of Congress Prints and Photographs Division [LC-USZ62-13026];
TEXT: Theodore Roosevelt. 1902. Quoted in Meyers, Robert Cornelius V. Theodore Roosevelt, Patriot and Statesman: The True Story of an Ideal American. Philadelphia: P.W. Ziegler & Co., 1902.

People going to work in
Washington, D.C.

Talk About It

COLLABORATE

Read the primary source quotation.
What does President Roosevelt
mean when he says, "we are the
Government"?

Working for the Future

Read what President George H. W. Bush said in his 1991 State of the Union address.

1 Inspect

Read President Bush's speech. What is he speaking about?

Underline the words you think are most important in the speech.

Discuss with a partner what President Bush thinks American citizens should do.

My Notes

_____

_____

_____

_____

_____

_____

_____

_____

_____

PRIMARY SOURCE

In Their Words... President George H. W. Bush

"We have within our reach the promise of a renewed America. We can find meaning and reward by serving some purpose higher than ourselves, a shining purpose, the illumination of a Thousand Points of Light. . .

. . . The problems before us may be different, but the key to solving them remains the same: it is the individual—the individual who steps forward. And the state of our Union is the union of each of us, one to the other—the sum of our friendships, marriages, families, and communities.

We all have something to give. So if you know how to read, find someone who can't. If you've got a hammer, find a nail. If you're not hungry, not lonely, not in trouble, seek out someone who is. Join the community of conscience. Do the hard work of freedom. That will define the state of our Union."

Copyright © McGraw-Hill Education
TEXT: George Herbert Walker Bush. "State of the Union Address." Washington, D.C., 29 January 1991.

George H. W. Bush was president of the United States from 1989–1992.

2 Find Evidence

Examine Reread the sentences, "Join the community of conscience. Do the hard work of freedom. That will define the state of our Union." Who does President Bush mean when he says, "the community of conscience?" Restate the sentences in your own words.

3 Make Connections

Talk Discuss with a partner why volunteering to help each other is important.

Connect to Now What can you do to help make your community stronger?

Explore Main Idea and Details

The **main idea** is the most important point the author makes about a topic. Key **details** tell about the main idea.

1. **Read the text once all the way through.**
   This will help you understand what the text is about.

2. **Reread the text and look for the most important idea.**
   This is the main idea.

3. **Look for an idea or example that tells about the main idea.**
   This is a detail.

4. **Look for another detail that tells about the main idea.**
   How many details can you find?

Based on the text you read, work with your class to complete the chart below based on President Bush's speech.

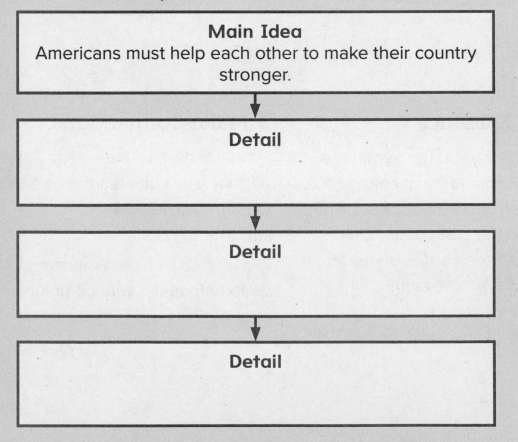

Main Idea
Americans must help each other to make their country stronger.

Detail

Detail

Detail

Investigate!

Read pages 216–223 in your Research Companion. Use your investigative skills to find details that tell about the main idea. This chart will help you organize your notes.

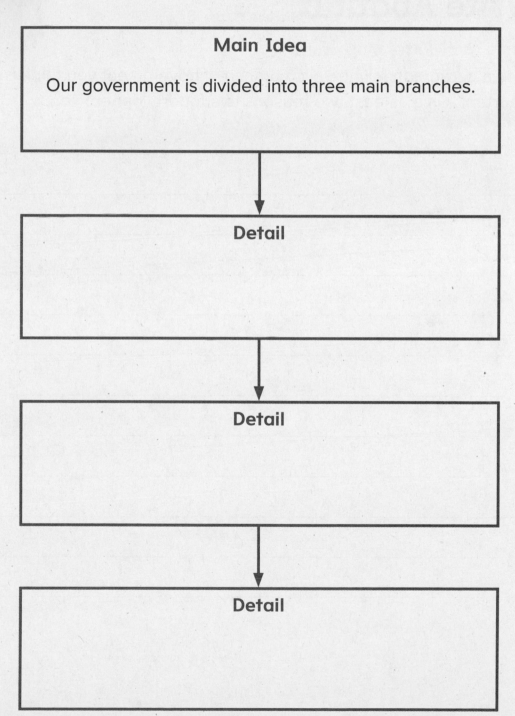

Main Idea

Our government is divided into three main branches.

↓

Detail

↓

Detail

↓

Detail

Think About It

Interpret

Review your research. Based on the information you have gathered, how do you think the three branches of government work together?

Write About It

Write and Cite Evidence

Write a paragraph telling which branch of government you think is most important. Give at least two reasons to support your opinion.

_____

_____

_____

_____

_____

_____

_____

_____

_____

_____

_____

Talk About It

Defend Your Claim

Share your writing with a partner who wrote about a different branch of government. Take turns talking about your opinions. Do you agree or disagree with your partner's opinion? Why?

Civics

Connect to the

Pull It Together

In what ways do you think the government can do a better job of working together? How can you help?

_____

_____

_____

Inquiry Project Notes

_____

_____

_____

_____

_____

_____

Lesson Outcomes

What Am I Learning?

In this lesson, you will use your investigative skills to learn about local governments in the United States.

Why Am I Learning It?

Reading and talking about local governments in the United States will help you understand why communities need governments.

How Will I Know That I Learned It?

You will be able to write a blog post about your local government and how it serves your community.

Talk About It

COLLABORATE

Look at the picture and read the caption on the next page. How can the word "lawmaker" help you know if this is the executive, judicial, or legislative branch of government?

A discussion by lawmakers

1 Inspect

Read the Primary Source quote. Who wrote this?

- **Circle** the subject of the page.
- **Underline** the important point John Marshall made about Native American nations.

My Notes

_____

_____

_____

_____

_____

_____

A Supreme Court Ruling

The Cherokee Native Americans lived in the southeastern United States. In the early 1800s, leaders in the state of Georgia tried to make the Cherokee people move from their homelands. Samuel Worcester, a friend of the Cherokee, lived on their land. Leaders in Georgia did not want Worcester to help the Cherokee. They passed a law saying that only Cherokee people could live on Cherokee land. Worcester was arrested for breaking this law and sent to prison.

Worcester asked the Supreme Court to hear his case. In 1832, the Supreme Court ruled the Georgia law was wrong. John Marshall was the Chief Justice of the Supreme Court.

PRIMARY SOURCE

In Their Words... Chief Justice John Marshall

"Indian Nations have always been considered as distinct, independent political communities, retaining their original natural rights, as the undisputed possessors of the soil.... The very term 'nation' so generally applied to them, means 'a people distinct from others.'"

—United States Supreme Court, 1832

He wrote that Native American nations are separate and independent from the United States. Justice Marshall said that states could not tell a Native American nation what to do. It was an important decision.

Troy Fletcher, executive director of the Yurok people, meets with state officials to talk about how to manage the Klamath River land.

2 Find Evidence

Reread the statement "Indian Nations have always been considered as distinct, independent political communities." What does the word *independent* mean? Name a word that has the same meaning as *independent*.

3 Make Connections

Talk Summarize John Marshall's comments in your own words.

COLLABORATE

Explore Summarizing

A **summary** is a short retelling of the important ideas of a text in your own words.

1. **Read the text once all the way through.**

2. **Look for the main ideas.**
   Authors often state the main ideas at the beginning or the end of a paragraph.

3. **Reread the text and look for key details.**
   These are the details that support the main idea.

4. **Tell what the text says in your own words.**
   Include main ideas and key details. A summary uses fewer words than the text.

COLLABORATE Based on the text you read, work with your class to add key details to the chart.

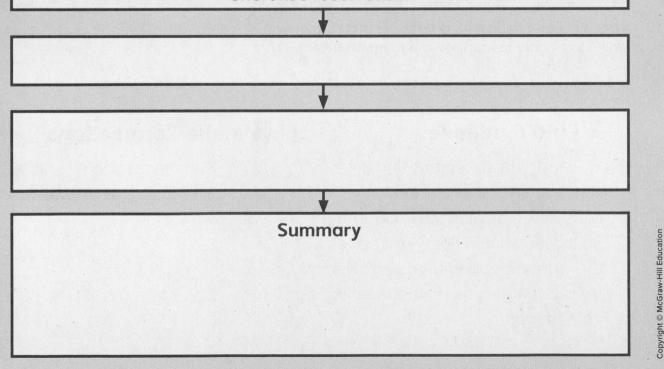

Leaders in Georgia arrested a non-Cherokee man living on a Cherokee reservation.

↓

↓

↓

Summary

Investigate!

Read pages 224–233 in your Research Companion. Use your investigative skills to look for the most important ideas to include in a summary. This chart will help you organize your notes.

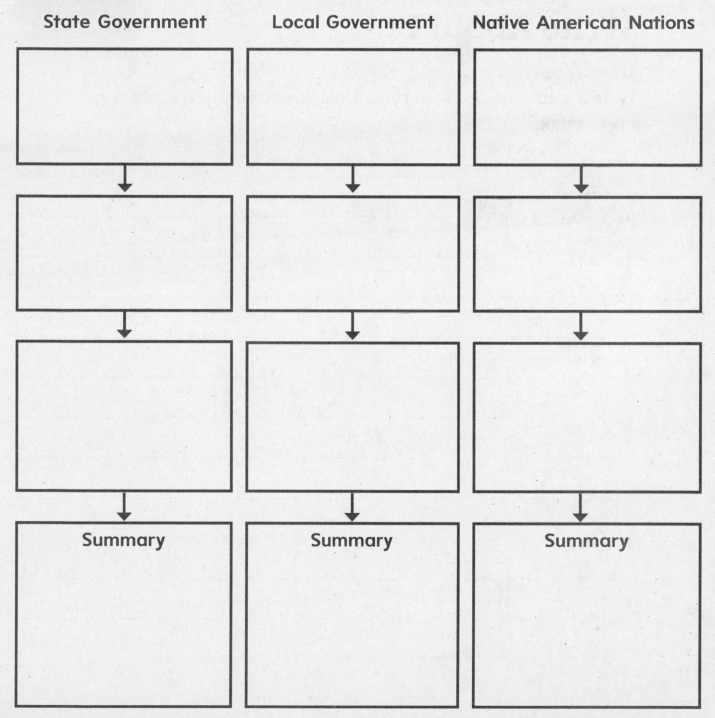

State Government	Local Government	Native American Nations
↓	↓	↓
↓	↓	↓
↓	↓	↓
Summary	Summary	Summary

Think About It

Contrast

Review your research on local government. How is it different from state and national governments? What kinds of services do local governments provide?

Write About It

Describe and Explain

Write a blog post describing your local government and explaining how it works.

_____

_____

_____

_____

_____

_____

_____

_____

_____

_____

Talk About It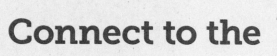

Explain

Share your blog post with a partner. Discuss the services local government provides in your community.

Civics

Connect to the

Pull It Together

How do local governments help communities?

_____

_____

_____

_____

_____

 Inquiry Project Notes

_____

_____

_____

_____

_____

Why Do We Follow Rules?

Lesson Outcomes

What Am I Learning?

In this lesson, you will use your investigative skills to learn about the rules and laws we must follow each day.

Why Am I Learning It?

Reading and talking about rules and laws will help you understand how they keep people in your community safe.

How Will I Know That I Learned It?

You will be able to write about some rules you follow and tell why they are important.

Talk About It

Look closely at the picture on the next page. What rules are being followed? Why are these rules needed in the community?

A crossing guard stops traffic for children walking to school.

1 Inspect

Read the title and look at the photographs. What do you think this text will be about?

- **Circle** the word *fine*. What clues help you figure out what it means?
- **Underline** clues that tell you why sports have rules about wearing safety equipment.
- **Highlight** what could happen to people who do not wear their seat belts.

My Notes

_____

_____

_____

_____

_____

_____

Safety Rules and Laws

Have you ever played football or soccer? These sports have rules that players must follow. In football, you must wear a helmet and pads to play. In soccer, you usually wear shin guards. Why do you think sports have these rules? The rules are to help keep the players safe.

The laws of your community also help keep you safe. Here's an example. People who wear seat belts are less likely to get hurt in a car accident. All states have laws about wearing a seat belt when riding in a car. If people do not wear one, they could get a ticket and pay a fine.

Seat belts keep us safe when we ride in a car.

Copyright © McGraw-Hill Education
PHOTO: Karen Town/E+/Getty Images

Car seats help keep babies safe while they are in a car.

Thousands of people are hurt in car accidents every year. Wearing a seat belt can mean the difference between life and death in an accident. Laws help make sure drivers and passengers stay safe by wearing a seat belt. Advertisements remind drivers and passengers to "Buckle Up." Police follow a "Click It or Ticket" program to protect people in cars. In many states, police officers can stop a driver if they see someone in the car not wearing a seat belt. A parent can be fined hundreds of dollars if a child is not buckled up! The police take car safety very seriously. You should too! Communities make rules and laws to keep people safe.

2 Find Evidence

Reread Why is it important to obey laws?

Examine What are the consequences of breaking seat belt laws?

3 Make Connections

Talk Why do police follow a "Click It or Ticket" program? Do you think this program will make people wear seat belts?

Explore Cause and Effect

A **cause** is why something happens. An **effect** is what happens. As you read, look for the causes of things.

1. **Read the text once all the way through.**
   This will help you understand what the text is about.

2. **Look for signal words such as *because* and *as a result*.**
   These clues often show a cause-and-effect relationship.

3. **Think about time order.**
   A cause happens before an effect.

4. **Ask why something happened.**
   This reason is the cause.

5. **Remember that a cause may have more than one effect.**

Based on the text you read, work with your class to complete the chart below.

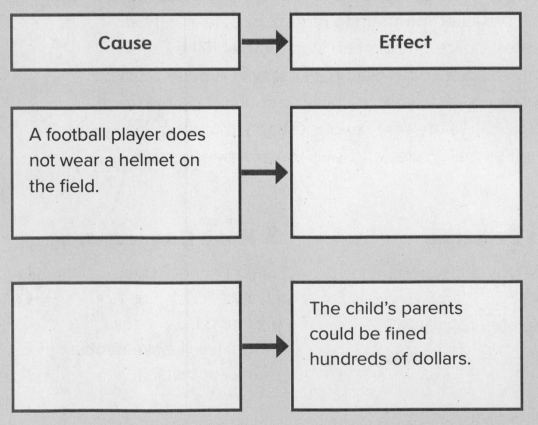

Cause	→	Effect
A football player does not wear a helmet on the field.	→	
	→	The child's parents could be fined hundreds of dollars.

Investigate!

Read pages 234–239 in your Research Companion. Use your investigative skills to look for text evidence that tells you what happened and why it happened. This chart will help you organize your notes.

Cause	→	Effect
	→	People in the community are safer.
Copying another student's homework is dishonest.	→	
A person breaks the law.	→	
	→	The cyclist's breaks the law and is not safe.
A person wants to be a good citizen.	→	

Think About It

Ask Yourself

Why do you think it is important to have rules and laws?

Write About It

Describe

What are some rules you follow at home? Describe two rules and what might happen if you do not follow them.

_____

_____

_____

_____

Explain

Based on what you have read in this lesson, why do you think it is important to have rules?

_____

_____

_____

_____

_____

_____

Talk About It

Discuss

Share your rules and the possible consequences if you do not follow them. How are your rules similar to or different from your partner's rules?

Civics

Connect to the

Pull It Together

Think about what you read in this lesson. How do rules and laws help us all live together?

_____

_____

_____

_____

_____

Inquiry Project Notes

_____

_____

_____

_____

_____

How Have Heroes Helped Communities?

Lesson Outcomes

What Am I Learning?

In this lesson, you will use your investigative skills to learn about real people who helped make their communities and the world better.

Why Am I Learning It?

Reading and talking about heroes will help you understand how people have solved problems.

How Will I Know That I Learned It?

You will be able to write about how people helped solve a problem in the world, nation, or their communities.

Talk About It

Look closely at the picture on the next page. Who is the most important person? Why do you think that?

Anne Hutchinson defends her actions during her trial in the colony of Massachusetts.

1 Inspect

Read the text all the way through.

Circle words you do not know.

Underline clues that tell you who Anne Hutchinson was.

Highlight clues that tell you where she lived.

Discuss with a partner why Anne Hutchinson was on trial.

My Notes

_____

_____

_____

_____

_____

_____

_____

Anne Hutchinson: A Hero for Freedom

Anne Hutchinson was born in England. Her father taught her to think for herself and to speak her mind. Anne sailed to Massachusetts with her family in 1634. They settled in Boston.

Anne was very religious. She began to have meetings in her home. At these meetings, she talked about religion. She believed God taught everyone, not just ministers and men. Her ideas were different from what the people in her community taught and believed.

The ministers who disagreed with Anne had her arrested. She was put on trial. During her trial, Anne Hutchinson stood by what she believed. She said only God could be her judge.

The court ordered Anne to leave the community. She left, but she never gave up her ideas or her right to think for herself.

PRIMARY SOURCE

In Their Words...
Anne Hutchinson

"Now, if you do condemn me for speaking what in my conscience I know to be truth I must commit myself unto the Lord."

—The Examination of Mrs. Anne Hutchinson at the Court at Newton, 1637

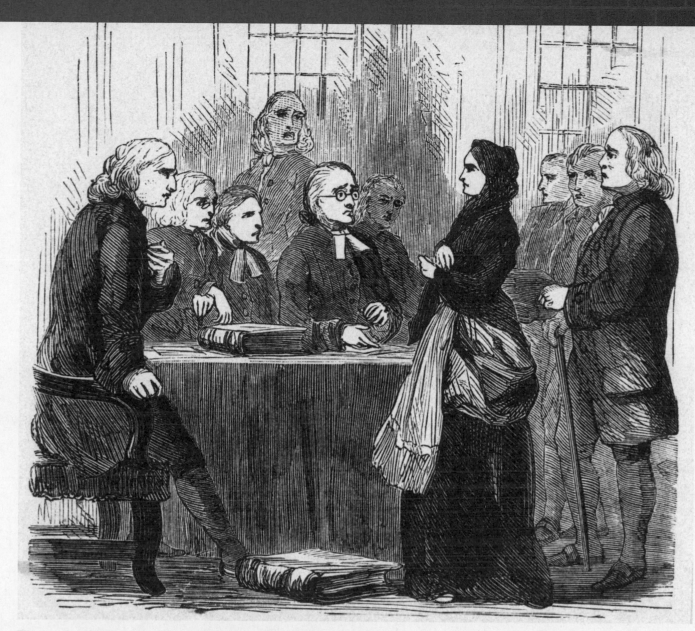

The court orders Anne Hutchinson to leave Boston.

2 Find Evidence

Reread the quote from Anne Hutchinson. How does this show her beliefs?

Underline words and sentences from the text that show how Anne stood up for her beliefs.

3 Make Connections

Talk Discuss with a partner why it is important to stand up for something you believe in.

Connect to Now Who is someone today who stands up for what he or she believes?

Explore Cause and Effect

A **cause** is why something happens. An **effect** is what happens. Thinking about causes and effects will help you understand events you read about.

1. **Read the text once all the way through.**
    This will help you understand what the text is about.

2. **Reread the text and look for something that tells you what happened.**
    This is the effect.

3. **Reread the text again and look for a detail that tells you *why* it happened.**
    This is the cause.

Based on the text you read, work with your class to complete the chart below.

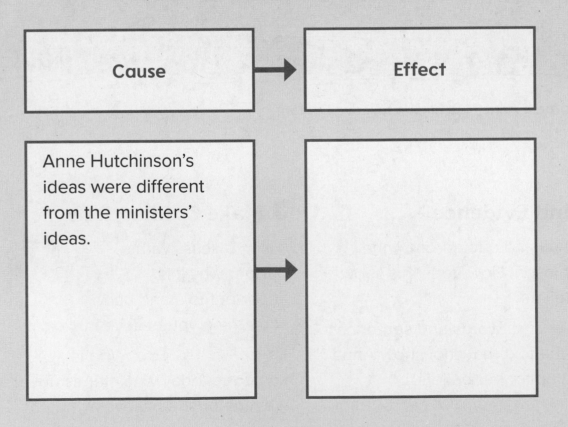

Cause	→	Effect

Anne Hutchinson's ideas were different from the ministers' ideas.

Investigate!

Read pages 240–249 in your Research Companion. Use your investigative skills to look for text evidence that tells you what heroes did and how their actions affected others. This chart will help you organize your notes.

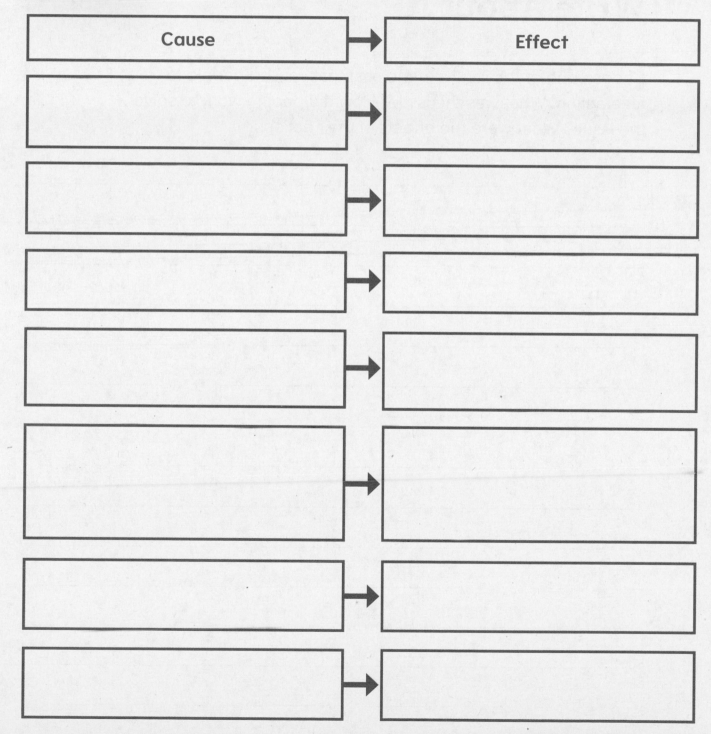

Cause	→	Effect
	→	
	→	
	→	
	→	
	→	
	→	
	→	

Think About It

Examine

Review your research. What are some problems in the past that people have tried to solve?

Write About It

Cause and Effect

Choose one of the issues in the past that caused people to take action. What was the issue? How did people work to solve the issue? What were the effects of their actions?

_____

_____

_____

_____

_____

_____

_____

_____

_____

_____

_____

Talk About It

Defend Your Claim

Share your paragraph with a partner. Discuss how the person or people you wrote about helped make the world a better place.

Civics Connect to the EQ

Pull It Together

In what ways can people work together to solve problems in a community?

_____

_____

_____

_____

_____

Inquiry Project Notes

_____

_____

_____

_____

_____

_____

Lesson 6

How Can You Help Build Strong Communities?

Lesson Outcomes

What Am I Learning?

In this lesson, you will use your investigative skills to explore how people strengthen their communities.

Why Am I Learning It?

Reading and talking about how people work together to take care of and improve their communities will help you understand how you can make a difference in your community.

How Will I Know That I Learned It?

You will be able to describe the characteristics of good leaders. You will also be able to write a paragraph proposing ways that you can help strengthen your community.

Talk About It

COLLABORATE

Read the quote from Dorothy Height. What is she suggesting that young people should do today? Why do you think that is?

Look closely at the photos. What are the young people doing? How do you think this activity helps the community?

Litter and other trash not only make a place look bad but also contribute to pollution and harm local plant and animal life. Pollution dirties the air, water, and land around us.

PRIMARY SOURCE

In Their Words... Dorothy Height

"I like to say to young people today, you are the beneficiaries of what a lot of people worked and gave their lives for. . . . And the important thing now is not to go it alone on your own, by yourself, but see how you will join with others. Get organized in how you will serve others and how you will help to move this forward."

—Civil Rights and Women's Rights Activist, NPR Interview, 2008

Building Community

We are all part of a community. When someone asks where we live, we might say the name of our town or state. We might also say we live in the United States. All three answers are correct.

A community can also be a neighborhood, a school, or even a classroom. A community is made up of different kinds of people. But the people in a community all share certain beliefs, rights, and responsibilities. Rights are things people can claim. Responsibilities are things people are expected to do.

Think about the different communities to which you belong. What kinds of beliefs, rights, and responsibilities do you share with other people in those communities? American citizens have many rights, like such as the freedom to share ideas. In exchange, they also have important responsibilities, such as obeying laws.

In a strong community, people try to do what is best for everybody. They follow rules and laws to help keep people safe. They work together to solve problems to improve life for everyone. Many people also volunteer to help make their community a better place for all who live there. To **volunteer** means to do a job or provide a service without pay.

What are some ways you can help make your community better?

Volunteers help clean their community's beach. Their work keeps trash out of the water as well as off the land.

2 Find Evidence

Reread How does the author say we can build stronger communities?

Underline clues that support what you think.

3 Make Connections

Talk Discuss with a partner what is happening in the photo. How is this an example of community service?

COLLABORATE

Write If you had an opportunity to volunteer in your community, what would you like to do and why?

Explore Drawing Conclusions

A **conclusion** is a decision you make about a topic. You use what you already know and information from what you read or observe to draw your conclusion. We draw conclusions when we read. We also draw conclusions from information we see in maps, charts, graphs, and photos.

1. **Read the title of the selection and captions for images.**
   This will help you know what the topic is.

2. **Read the text all the way through and look closely at images.**
   This will help you understand important ideas about the topic.

3. **Think about what you read or saw.**
   Ask: What information do the text and images give about the topic? What do I already know about the topic?

4. **Draw a conclusion.**
   Use information from the text as well as what you already know to draw a conclusion about the topic.

COLLABORATE   Based on the text, work with your class to draw a conclusion about what makes a strong community. Then work with your class to complete the chart below.

What Makes a Strong Community	
Text Clues and What I Already Know	Conclusions

Investigate!

Read pages 250–257 in your Research Companion. Use your investigative skills to look for text evidence that tells you how citizens can build strong communities. This chart will help you organize your notes.

Text Clues and What I Already Know	Conclusions
Becoming a good citizen:	How to build a strong community:
Characteristics of good leaders:	
Problems in my community:	
Ways to make a difference in my community:	

Think About It

Identify

Review your research and the problems discussed in the lesson. Think about a problem that affects your community right now.

Write About It

Explain

Write a paragraph describing a problem that exists in your community today. How would you solve the problem?

_____

_____

_____

_____

_____

_____

Talk About It

COLLABORATE

Discuss and Compare

Share your paragraph with a partner. Compare your problems and solutions. Ask for a different solution to the problem you wrote about. Offer a different solution for your partner's problem. If time permits, discuss the benefits and drawbacks for each solution. Which solution might best address each problem, and why?

Civics

Connect to the EQ

Pull It Together

Remember that citizens have rights and responsibilities. Think about how these ideas relate to volunteering and community service. Why is community service an important part of being a citizen?

_____

_____

_____

Inquiry Project Notes

_____

_____

_____

_____

_____

Why Do Governments and Citizens Need Each Other?

Inquiry Project

Creating a Classroom Constitution

For this project, you will work with your class to write a constitution that sets classroom rules.

Complete Your Project

☐ Decide on a purpose for your classroom constitution.

☐ List rules that everyone must follow.

☐ Determine the consequences for breaking rules.

☐ Write a classroom constitution that explains the rules everyone must follow and the consequences for breaking a rule.

Share Your Project

☐ Read the constitution aloud.

☐ Review the rules and the consequences for breaking them.

☐ Explain how the rules were chosen, and discuss their purpose.

☐ Sign the constitution, and promise to follow it.

☐ Post the constitution in your classroom.

Think about the work you did in this chapter and on your project. Use the questions below to help guide your thoughts.

1. How did you determine the purpose for your class constitution?

_____

2. What compromises did the class make? _____

_____

3. Are the consequences for breaking the rules fair?_____

_____

Chapter Connections

Use pictures, words, or both to reflect on what you learned in this chapter.

The most interesting thing I learned:

Something I learned from a classmate:

A connection I can make with my own life:

Economics of Communities

How Do People in a Community Meet Their Wants and Needs?

In this chapter, you will learn about the resources businesses use to make our economy strong. You will also explore how businesses make money and why they spend it. With a team, you will work on a chapter project to write a blog about a local business and how it helps your community.

Talk About It   COLLABORATE

Discuss with a partner the questions you have about how businesses in your area earn money and make a profit.

Copyright © McGraw-Hill Education
PHOTO: gopixa/iStock/Getty Images

People buy food and other goods at a supermarket.

Blogging About a Local Business

In this project, you will work with a small group to create a blog about a local business and describe how it helps your community.

- [ ] **Select** a local business in your community.
- [ ] **Create** a list of questions to ask the business owner. Ask about the owner's background, the company's resources and goods or services, and how the business helps the community meet its needs.
- [ ] **Conduct** an interview with the owner of the business.
- [ ] **Determine** what information should be included on the blog and how you will present it.
- [ ] **Write** a blog on the business you selected, using the information you have gathered. Add pictures, charts, or graphs to support your ideas.
- [ ] **Share** your blog with your class and have them comment on your findings.

Write down any research questions you have that will help you plan your project. You can add questions as you carry out your research.

_____

_____

Complete this chapter's Word Rater. Write notes as you learn more about each word.

benefits

My Notes

☐ Know It!

_____

☐ Heard It!

_____

☐ Don't Know It!

_____

capital resource

My Notes

☐ Know It!

_____

☐ Heard It!

_____

☐ Don't Know It!

_____

economy

My Notes

☐ Know It!

_____

☐ Heard It!

_____

☐ Don't Know It!

_____

entrepreneur

My Notes

☐ Know It!

_____

☐ Heard It!

_____

☐ Don't Know It!

_____

export

My Notes

☐ Know It!

_____

☐ Heard It!

_____

☐ Don't Know It!

_____

human capital

My Notes

☐ Know It!

_____

☐ Heard It!

_____

☐ Don't Know It!

_____

human resource

My Notes

☐ Know It!

_____

☐ Heard It!

_____

☐ Don't Know It!

_____

import

My Notes

☐ Know It!

_____

☐ Heard It!

_____

☐ Don't Know It!

_____

scarcity

My Notes

☐ Know It!

_____

☐ Heard It!

_____

☐ Don't Know It!

_____

specialize

My Notes

☐ Know It!

_____

☐ Heard It!

_____

☐ Don't Know It!

_____

Lesson 1

How Can Communities Use Their Resources?

Lesson Outcomes

What Am I Learning?

In this lesson, you will use your investigative skills to find out what kinds of resources businesses use.

Why Am I Learning It?

Reading and talking about resources will help you understand how businesses in the United States provide goods and services.

How Will I Know That I Learned It?

You will be able to describe a business in your community that is affected by the environment.

Talk About It

Look closely at the photographs. In what type of community do you think each industry takes place? How do you know?

Different communities have important industries.

1 Inspect

Read the title. What do you think this text will be about?

- **Circle** the names of the major crops grown in the United States.
- **Underline** details that explain how agriculture affects the economy of the country and specific regions.

My Notes

_____

_____

_____

_____

_____

_____

_____

_____

_____

_____

Agriculture Depends on Resources

Agriculture is a major industry in the United States. About half of the corn used throughout the world is produced in the United States. The region is ideal for agriculture because of its fertile land and its rivers. Other major products include soybeans, wheat, cotton, fruits, vegetables, and dairy products.

Most corn is grown in the Midwest. Other Midwest crops include soybeans, wheat, potatoes, pumpkins, tomatoes, lentils, and oats. The Northeast produces crops such as apples, potatoes, cranberries, and tomatoes. The Southeast is known for peanuts, rice, oranges, sweet potatoes, and tomatoes. In the Southwest, farmers grow lettuce, potatoes, chili peppers, and rice. States in the West produce many crops including potatoes, grapes, nuts, strawberries, and tomatoes.

The United States exports agricultural products to countries around the world. Agriculture also benefits every U.S. region.

Harvesting tomatoes

2 Find Evidence

Reread the text. How do farmers depend on the land to be successful?

Examine the second paragraph. Identify two crops that are grown in more than one U.S. region.

3 Make Connections

Talk with a partner about how agriculture may help the economy of a region and the country.

Explore Main Idea and Details

The **main idea** is what the text is about. **Details** tell you more about the main idea.

1. **Read the text all the way through.**
   This will help you understand what the text is about.

2. **Reread the text and look for the most important point.**
   The most important point is the main idea. Look for a sentence that states the main idea.

3. **Look for ideas that tell you more about the most important point.**
   These ideas are the details.

Based on the text you read, work with your class to complete the chart.

Main Idea	Details
Agriculture is a major industry in the United States.	

Investigate!

Read pages 266–273 in your Research Companion. Use your investigative skills to look for text evidence that tells you how businesses use resources. This chart will help you organize your notes.

Main Idea	Details

Think About It

Examine

Based on your research, what types of businesses are found in your community?

Write About It

Describe

Write a paragraph describing a business in your community that depends on the resources found there. Give reasons to support your answer.

_____

_____

_____

_____

_____

_____

_____

_____

_____

_____

_____

_____

Talk About It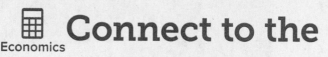

Give Reasons

Talk to a classmate who chose a different business. Take turns discussing your business and reasons why you chose that business. Do you agree or disagree with your partner's reasons?

Economics

Connect to the

Pull It Together

How do businesses in your community use resources to help people meet their needs?

_____

_____

_____

_____

 Inquiry Project Notes

_____

_____

_____

_____

_____

_____

Lesson 2

How Do Businesses and Communities Provide Goods and Services?

Lesson Outcomes

What Am I Learning?

In this lesson, you will use your investigative skills to find out how businesses and communities provide goods and services.

Why Am I Learning It?

Reading and talking about how businesses and communities provide goods and services will help you better understand where the goods and services in your own life come from.

How Will I Know That I Learned It?

You will be able to write a paragraph explaining what goods and services you would imagine providing to your community in a successful business.

Talk About It

COLLABORATE

Look closely at the photo. What are these people doing? What kind of business is this? How can you tell?

Workers in a business sell goods and services.

The American Dream

1 Inspect

Read the article "The American Dream" and the Primary Source quote.

Underline examples of success in the article.

Circle words in the quote you do not know.

My Notes

_____

_____

_____

_____

_____

_____

_____

_____

_____

_____

_____

Many people want the "American Dream." They want to have the chance to succeed—to get a good job, own a home, or run their own business. The economy of the United States is based on the success of its citizens. People must have jobs and earn money in a successful economy. Businesses create jobs. They hire people to make and sell their goods and services.

PRIMARY SOURCE

In Their Words... James Truslow Adams

"The American Dream is that dream of a land in which life should be better and richer and fuller for everyone, with opportunity for each according to ability or achievement."

—James Truslow Adams, *The Epic of America*

All the workers in a business help the business succeed.

Workers are important to any business. A business cannot operate without people doing their jobs. A good business will have many different kinds of workers. They may have different skills. Some workers will make the goods. Others will provide a service. When people work together, it makes the business a better place to work. The work they do allows the business to earn money. This way, both the workers and the business are successful. Success gives people the opportunity to improve their lives.

2 Find Evidence

Reread the quote. Who does the historian James Truslow Adams think should benefit from the American Dream?

Underline the three words describing what life should be.

Circle the words describing what opportunity should be based on.

3 Make Connections

Talk Discuss with a partner different ways in which a worker's ability and achievement help the worker and the business succeed.

Explore Making Inferences

When you read, you often make inferences about the text. An **inference** is a decision you make about the meaning of the text. To make an inference, you can do the following.

1. **Read the text once all the way through.**
   This will help you understand what the text is about.

2. **Think about what you read.**
   An author may not always tell you everything. What questions do you have?

3. **Think about what you already know about this topic.**

4. **Make a decision about the text.**
   Base your decision on what you know and what you read.

COLLABORATE

Based on the text you read, work with your class to complete the chart below.

Text Clues and What I Already Know	Inferences
James Truslow Adams says that the American Dream is of a better life for everyone according to ability or achievement. I know:	Adams means that:

Investigate!

Read pages 274–281 in your Research Companion. Use your investigative skills to make inferences about how businesses and communities provide goods and services. This chart will help you organize your notes.

Text Clues and What I Already Know	Inferences
Manufacturing goods uses capital resources and human resources. I know:	This means that:
Services have value to the people who use them. I know:	This means that:
Communities need strong, healthy businesses to survive. I know:	This means that:

Think About It

Examine

Based on your research, how do you think businesses are able to earn money to make a profit?

Write About It

Identify

What kinds of goods or services do you think people in your community would use?

_____

_____

_____

_____

Write and Cite Evidence

Imagine that you want to start a business in your community. Describe what kind of business you would start and what kinds of goods or services you would provide. Tell why you think your imaginary business would be successful.

_____

_____

_____

_____

_____

_____

Talk About It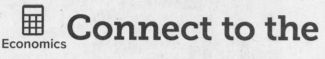

Explain

Share your business idea with a partner. Discuss how the goods and services you and your partner identified would benefit your community.

Economics

Connect to the EQ

Look at Our Community

How can successful businesses help people in a community meet their needs and wants?

_____

_____

_____

_____

_____

_____

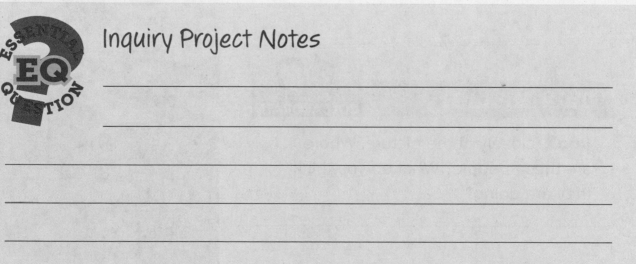

Inquiry Project Notes

_____

_____

_____

_____

Lesson Outcomes

What Am I Learning?

In this lesson, you will use your investigative skills to learn how markets and trade provide people with what they want and need.

Why Am I Learning It?

Reading and talking about markets and trade will help you understand how the items in your life got to you from other places.

How Will I Know That I Learned It?

You will be able to write a story telling how an item in your classroom came to be there.

Talk About It
COLLABORATE

Look closely at the picture. Where are these people? What do you think they are doing?

Buyers and sellers at a marketplace

1 Inspect

Read the title. What do you think this text will be about?

Circle words you do not know.

Underline clues that tell you:

- **What** is a market?
- **What** kinds of markets are there?
- **Why** are markets helpful?

My Notes

_____

_____

_____

_____

_____

_____

_____

_____

What Do We Mean When We Say Market?

A market is a place where things are bought and sold. You may have visited an outdoor farmers' market before. Local growers bring fresh fruits and vegetables to the market to sell. People from the community come to the market to buy these goods.

A market can also be a store inside a building. The store may have some local things for sale, but many of the items came from other places. Canned and jarred foods may have come from other parts of the United States. Toys and electronics most likely came from other countries.

A market is not always a physical place. It can also be an imaginary area where trade happens. For example, the American housing market is not an actual place. It refers to the buying and selling of all houses in America.

A market can be a physical place where people buy fruits and vegetables.

The stock market is another example of a market that's not an actual place. When people buy stocks, they buy a small ownership in a company. Companies sell stocks to raise money.

All markets help people get the things they want or need. First, sellers bring goods or services to a market, which may be a real place or an imaginary one. Then, they sell their goods or services. Next, the sellers receive money from the buyers. Finally, the sellers become buyers. They use the money they received to buy different goods.

Stock prices often go up and down throughout the day.

2 Find Evidence

Reread How can someone be both a buyer and a seller?

Draw a box around the sentences that provide the answer.

3 Make Connections

Talk Look at the photograph COLLABORATE on page 265. What type of market does it show? How do you know?

Explore Sequence

Writers use **sequence** to show the order in which events happen.

1. **Read the text all the way through.**
   This will help you understand what the text is about.

2. **Look for clues that tell you the order of events.**
   Pay close attention to the order in which the writer presents facts and ideas. Words such as *first*, *next*, *then*, and *finally* show time order. Numbered steps can also show time order.

3. **Describe the sequence.**
   Use time order words or a numbered list to show the order in which things happen.

COLLABORATE
How does a seller become a buyer? Based on the text you read, work with your class to complete the chart below.

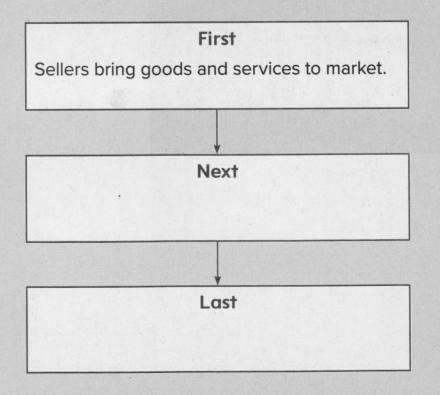

First
Sellers bring goods and services to market.

↓

Next

↓

Last

Investigate!

Read pages 282–287 in your Research Companion. Use your investigative skills to look for text evidence that tells you the sequence of events of how people get what they need and why that makes the economy stronger. Use the vocabulary word in each box to guide you.

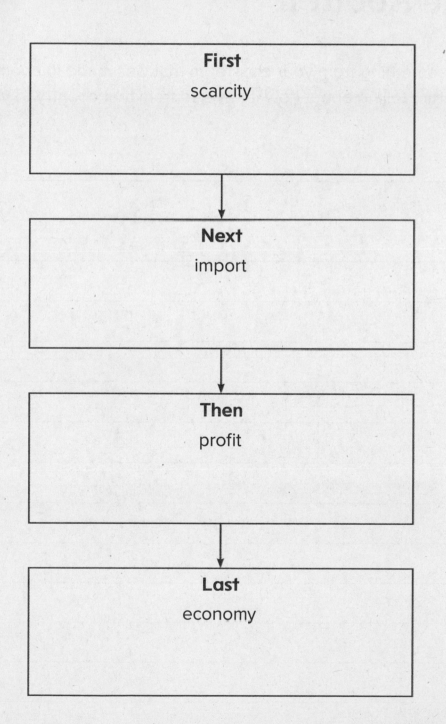

First

scarcity

Next

import

Then

profit

Last

economy

Think About It

Examine

Where were the things in your classroom made? Look for labels showing the countries where they were manufactured.

Write About It

Describe

Choose something from your classroom that was made in another country. Write a story telling about how it traveled from that country to your classroom.

_____

_____

_____

_____

_____

_____

_____

_____

_____

_____

_____

_____

Talk About It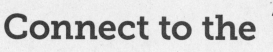

Explain

Share your story with a partner. Discuss how and why objects made in one part of the world end up in another place.

Economics

Connect to the

Look at Our Community

How does trade help the people in your community meet their wants and needs? How is your story an example of this?

_____

_____

_____

_____

_____

_____

 Inquiry Project Notes

_____

_____

_____

_____

What Makes a Community's Economy Change?

Lesson Outcomes

What Am I Learning?

In this lesson, you will use your investigative skills to explore how buying and selling goods and services have changed over time.

Why Am I Learning It?

Reading and talking about these changes will help you understand how sales and shopping work in communities today.

How Will I Know That I Learned It?

You will be able to write and talk about the goods and services you would have used in your community one hundred years ago.

Talk About It

COLLABORATE

Look closely at the photo on the next page. Are these people buying goods or services? Who provides them?

When you buy a ticket to a show, you're paying for entertainment. Other people perform in concerts, plays, and movies for your enjoyment!

At an amusement park, people buy tickets to see shows and ride on rides.

Shopping Long Ago and Today

Long ago, most towns had only a few small stores. Each store carried only a few different items. Most of the items were made nearby. Items that came from far away were expensive and not easy to get. Customers who walked to a store could buy only a few items at a time. Customers are people who buy goods and services. Customers who rode in wagons could bring home more food, clothing, tools, and other items. Most people paid for goods in cash. Some traded their own goods for others.

In the past, most people shopped in small stores in their communities. They might buy food at one store, tools at another, and clothing at another.

Today, people can buy goods from their computer and telephone. The goods arrive on the doorstep or in the mailbox!

Today, customers have more choices among goods. The same items are available all year. Many customers drive to the store. This makes it easier to reach stores farther away. People can also bring many things home at one time.

Customers use the Internet to buy goods from stores that have websites. Online shopping allows people to buy goods from stores in other states and countries. Goods ordered online are shipped to people's homes and businesses.

People have many ways to pay for goods and services. They can use cash, checks, and credit cards. Credit cards let customers charge goods that they must pay for later.

2 Find Evidence

Reread the text. How do changes in how people shop affect the local economy?

Draw a box around clues that support what you think.

3 Make Connections

Talk Discuss with a partner why people might shop online. What goods and services do they get online?

Explore Comparing and Contrasting

To **compare** means to identify how things are alike. To **contrast** means to identify how things are different.

1. **Read the text all the way through.**

2. **Reread the text. Look for things that have stayed the same over time.**

3. **Reread each section of text. Look for things that have changed over time.**

Using the text, work with your class to complete the chart below.

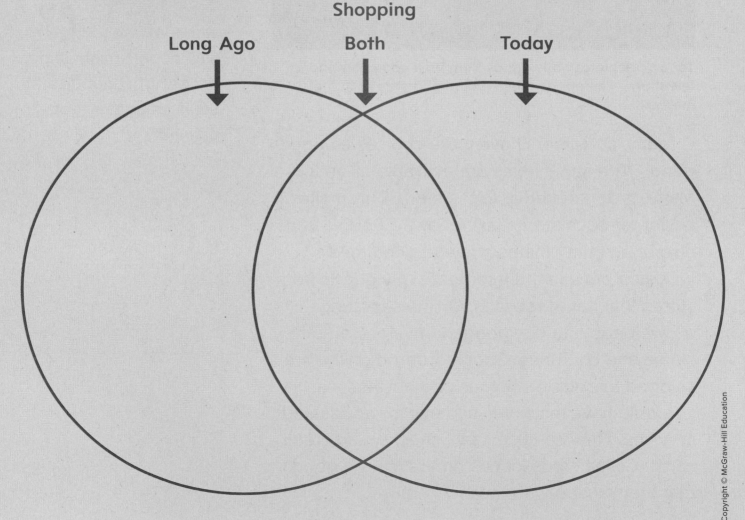

Shopping

Long Ago   Both   Today

Investigate!

Read pages 288–293 in your Research Companion. Use your investigative skills to look for text evidence that tells you how goods and services have changed over time. This chart will help you organize your notes.

Goods and Services

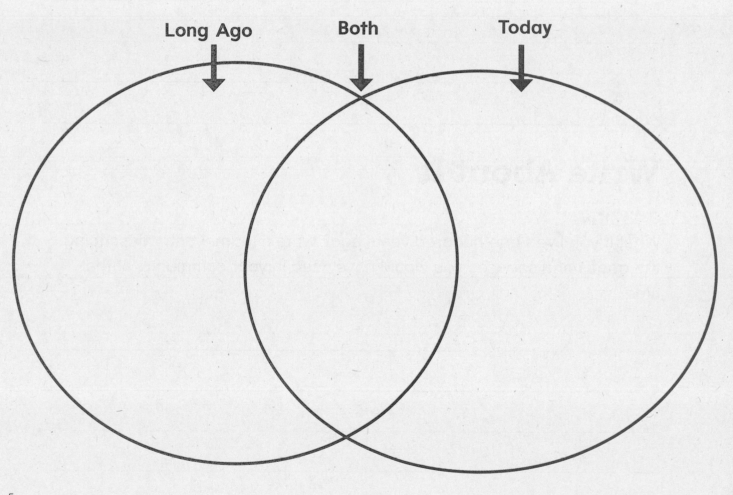

Long Ago   Both   Today

Think About It

Examine

Based on your research, what goods and services have businesses in the United States provided?

_____

_____

_____

_____

_____

Write About It

Imagine

What if you lived one hundred years ago? Write a journal entry describing the goods and services you would have used in your community at that time.

_____

_____

_____

_____

_____

_____

Talk About It

Discuss

Share your paragraph with a partner. Discuss how the goods and services in your community have changed over time. How do you think those changes have shaped your community?

Economics

Connect to the

Evaluate

What are the benefits and drawbacks to the ways people make, sell, and buy goods and services in your community today?

_____

_____

_____

_____

 Inquiry Project Notes

_____

_____

_____

_____

_____

_____

Lesson 5

How Can You Use Money Wisely?

Lesson Outcomes

What Am I Learning?

In this lesson, you will use your investigative skills to explore how people choose to use money.

Why Am I Learning It?

Reading and talking about how people make choices with money will help you make good choices about using your money.

How Will I Know That I Learned It?

You will be able to write a list of questions that you should ask yourself about using your money.

Talk About It

COLLABORATE

Look closely at the picture on the next page. What do you think the children are discussing? What choices do they have to make? How will they decide?

Thinking before you buy helps you make good spending choices.

Good Money Choices

1 Inspect

Read the title. What do you think this text will be about?

- **Underline** questions you should ask before buying something.

My Notes

_____

_____

_____

_____

_____

_____

_____

_____

_____

_____

_____

_____

_____

How do you decide how to use your money? Do you save some or spend it all? When you spend money, do you buy something you need or something you want? Do you take time to think about your purchase before making it? It is important to ask yourself some questions before you buy something. You might ask: Is this something I really need? Is the most expensive item the best choice? Will a less expensive item be just as good? Do I have enough money? Should I save my money for something else I really need or want?

PRIMARY SOURCE

In Their Words... Benjamin Franklin

"Beware of little expenses, a small leak will sink a great ship."

—*Poor Richard's Almanack*

People spend money on things that they need and on things that they want.

Earning money takes time and effort. So, people need to make good choices about how to use their money. They might save, donate, or spend some of their money.

People buy things they need, such as food. They buy other things because they want them, like games and toys. People need to think about the costs and **benefits** of buying an item because every choice involves a tradeoff. It's easy to spend money on a want without thinking about it. But that could mean they may not have enough to buy something they really need later.

2 Find Evidence

Reread What is the difference between a want and a need?

Examine the text. What examples does it give of wants and needs?

3 Make Connections

Talk With a partner, discuss Benjamin Franklin's statement. What does it mean? Do you agree? Why or why not?

Explore Main Idea and Details

The **main idea** is the most important idea of a paragraph, a section, or an article. **Details** tell more about the main idea. When you read, it is helpful to focus on the main ideas.

1. **Read the text all the way through.**
   This will help you understand what the text is about.

2. **Think about what you read.**
   Ask yourself: *What is it about? What is the author trying to say?*

3. **In each section of the text, look for a main idea.**
   Section titles will give you clues. Sometimes the first or last paragraph in a section contains the main idea.

4. **Look for key details that tell more about the main ideas.**

Based on the text you read, work with your class to complete the chart.

	Main Idea	Details
Wise Money Choices		

Investigate!

Read pages 294–301 in your Research Companion. Use your investigative skills to look for text evidence that tells you the main ideas and their supporting details. This chart will help you organize your notes.

	Main Idea	Details
Using Money		
Earning Money to Help Others		
Making Economic Choices		
Building Your Own Capital		

Think About It

Examine

Based on your research, what will help you make wise choices about using money?

Write About It

Write and Cite Evidence

What questions should you consider before you buy something? Use details from the text to explain your response.

_____

_____

_____

_____

_____

_____

_____

_____

_____

_____

_____

_____

Talk About It

Discuss

Compare your list with a partner. Discuss why these questions are important. Which questions do you and your partner think are most important?

Connect to the **EQ**

Look at Our Community

How does making good money choices help people in your community meet their needs?

_____

_____

_____

_____

_____

 Inquiry Project Notes

_____

_____

_____

_____

_____

How Do People in a Community Meet Their Wants and Needs?

Blogging About a Local Business

For this project, you will write a blog about a local business and explain how it helps your community.

Complete Your Project

☐ Identify a local business in your community that you would like to learn more about.

☐ List questions you could ask the owner of the business.

☐ Conduct an interview with the owner.

☐ Write a blog about the business.

Share Your Project

☐ Name the business you describe in your blog.

☐ Tell what you have learned. Explain how the business helps your community.

☐ Answer any questions your class might have.

Think about the work you did in this chapter and on your project. Use the questions below to help guide your thoughts.

1. Why did you choose the business that you researched?

_____

2. How did you conduct your research? Is there anything you would do differently next time? _____

_____

3. How did you make sure that your sources were reliable? _____

_____

Chapter Reflections

Use pictures, words, or both to reflect on what you learned in this chapter.

The most interesting thing I learned:

Something I learned from a classmate:

A connection I can make with my own life:

Studying the Stars

CHARACTERS

Narrator	**Theo**
	(Ava's younger brother)
Dad	
	Beth
Mom	
Ava	*(Ava's friend)*

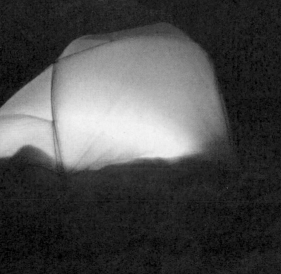

Narrator: Ava's family is camping for the weekend. They are up in the mountains. Without city lights, it is easier to see what's in the night sky. Ava's Dad shows her a group of stars that form a shape in the sky.

Dad: *(pointing to the sky)* There's the Big Dipper. Can you see it?

Ava: I think so. It looks like a scoop.

Mom: Yes. Look at the two stars on the outer edge of the dipper. You can use those two stars to find the North Star.

Ava: I think I see it. Is it that bright one?

Dad: Yes, that's it.

Theo: I'm not sure I see it.

Ava: *(pointing to help her brother)* Look over there. It's brighter than the other stars.

Dad: The North Star is also called Polaris.

Ava: Wow! There are so many stars. I wonder what else is out there.

Theo: Aliens!

(Ava at home with her family)

Narrator: Ava is excited about looking at the stars. At school, Ava learns about astronomy. She finds out that she can look at stars through a telescope. Ava has an idea. She tells her family about it at dinner.

Ava: I've been thinking about how much I like looking at the stars. I'm going to need a telescope.

Dad: A telescope? Really? Is that something you need or just something you want?

Ava: I guess it's just something I want. But if I'm going to be an astronomer, I want to start studying the stars right now.

Theo: What's an astronomer?

Mom: Someone who studies the stars and planets in the universe.

Ava: That's right. That's what I want to do.

Dad: That's great, but do you know what a telescope costs?

Ava: Not really.

Dad: Then you need to find out. Our budget right now doesn't include buying a telescope. You might need to save up some money if you want one.

Theo: What's a budget?

Mom: It's a plan for how we spend our income.

Theo: What's an income?

Mom: It's the money we receive for working.

Ava: Hmmm. I need a plan.

Narrator: After dinner, Ava searches the Internet. She finds out that a new telescope can cost a lot of money. Much more than she expected. Then she asks Mom for help.

Ava: I found out how much telescopes cost, and I need a plan.

Mom: Is a telescope that important to you?

Ava: Yes. I want to study the stars. Maybe I'll make an important discovery someday.

Mom: Is it more important than the new game you wanted to buy?

Ava: Yes, I think so.

Mom: Well . . . you can always save the money you get for your birthday.

Ava: Good idea, but I'll need more.

Mom: How about doing some extra chores around the house? We could probably pay you a little.

Ava: Really? That would be great! What can I do?

Mom: Let's make a list of jobs you could do.

Ava: OK. I'll get my tablet.

Mom: Let's see, in addition to your normal chores, you can help me walk Max.

Ava: OK. How about the recycling? I could take care of that every week.

Mom: That sounds good. And Theo could use your help to learn his spelling words.

Ava: I guess I could do that.

Mom: There are some jobs that we only need help with at certain times— like raking leaves and pulling weeds.

Ava: I'll put those on the list.

(A few days later, at Ava's home)

Narrator: Ava comes home from walking Max, the family dog. Her friend Beth is waiting for her.

Beth: Wow, you've been busy!

Ava: Yes, I walk Max every day—with my mom—but it's my job to clean up after him.

Beth: Yuck!

Ava: My mom and I made a list of jobs I can do. It keeps me busy.

Beth: How much money have you saved for your telescope?

Ava: Well, not much yet. It will take a while to save what I need.

Beth: How long?

Ava: I'm not sure, but I think it will be several months. I already have some birthday money saved that I can use.

Beth: You must really want a telescope!

Ava: I do! It's worth giving up some of my time to earn extra money. I can't wait to go camping again and look at the stars through a telescope!

Beth: Can I come?

Ava: Sure!

Talk About It

Talk Tell a partner about something you really wanted. What did you give up to get it? What were the benefits of getting the item?

Glossary

A

apartheid a system of racial inequality and segregation

artifact an object that was used by people in the past

atmosphere the layer of gases that surround a planet, such as Earth

B

benefits something that helps a person

boycott a special kind of protest where people decide to stop doing, using, or buying something

C

capital resource the tools and machines that people use to make products or provide services

citizen a person who lives in a community or is a member of a country

climate the weather a place has over a long period of time

community the place where people live, work, and play

compromise an agreement that people make when they have different ideas

culture the values, beliefs, and other ways of life shared by a group of people

D

decade ten years

deforestation the loss of forests

drought a shortage of water due to lack of rainfall

economy the way a country uses its money, goods, resources, and services

ecosystem the plants and animals that live in a particular place

elevation how high an area of land is above sea level

endangered an animal that is at risk of becoming extinct

entrepreneur a person who starts and runs a business

erosion the wearing away of Earth's surface over a period of time

ethnic group a group of people who share the same culture

executive branch the part of government that makes sure that laws are carried out and followed

expedition a journey, especially by a group of people, for a specific purpose

export to send goods to another country to sell

extinct a type of animal that has no more living members

federal national

folktale a story handed down over the years

H

habitat the home of an animal or plant

heritage a person's background or tradition

hero a person who helps make the world better for other people

human capital the skills and knowledge a person has to do a job

human resource the people who work for a business or person

humidity a measure of how much moisture is in the air

hydroelectric dam a type of dam, or barrier, that turns the energy of moving water into electric power

import to bring in goods from another country to sell

innovation a new idea, piece of equipment, or method

judicial branch the part of government that decides what the laws mean

jury a group of citizens who are chosen to decide a legal case

justice treating people fairly and equally under law

landform a physical feature of the land, such as mountains, valleys, and coasts

legislative branch the part of government that makes the laws

M

monument a building, statue, or other structure that honors a person, place, or event in history

N

natural disaster an event that occurs in nature that damages the environment and may harm living things, such as a hurricane, earthquake, or tornado

natural resource something found in nature that people use

O

oral tradition stories and poems that are spoken rather than written

ozone layer a layer in the Earth's atmosphere that absorbs the sun's harmful rays and helps keep Earth's temperature controlled

peninsula a piece of land mostly surrounded by water

pioneer a person who settled in a wilderness area

population the number of people who live in one place

precipitation water that falls to the ground as rain, snow, sleet, or hail

public services a service supplied to all members of a community

region an area of land with certain features that make it different from other areas

rights some things that are due to everyone

scarcity when there is a limited amount of a good or service that many people want

specialize to focus on providing a particular product or service

strait a narrow waterway connecting two larger bodies of water

T

taxes money collected by a government

technology the use of knowledge to invent new tools that make life easier and solve problems

tolerance accepting something different from your own beliefs and customs

V

volunteer to do a job or provide a service without pay

points (such as diamonds, checks, or checked boxes); use round ones instead but not "hollow" round bullets. The scanner will read those as the letter "o." Write out words for symbols, such as "and" instead of "&" and "percent" instead of "%."

Keep your overall formatting simple. Use white space to your advantage for separating sections of your résumé rather than boxes or lines. Do not use a newsletter format, as this will confuse the scanning software.

When sending a résumé to be scanned, provide as clean a copy as possible; preferably one fresh off a laser printer and sent in a flat envelope. Do not print your scannable résumé on fancy paper that has a marble appearance or specks. Try to avoid faxing your scannable résumé whenever possible, as fax machines tend to create marks on the printout that can cause problems for the OCR reader (optical character recognition, the program that deciphers scannable résumés).

Mary B. Nemnich and Fred E. Jandt provide the following tips for scannable résumés in their book, *Cyber Space Résumé Kit* (Jist Works, 2001):

- Keep layout simple.
- Keep fonts simple.
- Keep your copy clean.
- Use good-quality paper.
- Send originals whenever possible.
- Use a high-quality photocopier for reproductions.

A Few Words about Keywords

Keywords should not be confused with your action verbs. Keywords are nouns or short phrases that describe your experience, educa-

tion, and other important information. Become familiar with your industry's "buzzwords" and incorporate them into your résumé. Keywords can be compiled as a list but can also be worked into the text of your résumé. The scanning software scans the entire résumé, so keywords will be picked up no matter where they are placed. Use synonyms wherever possible to increase your chances of getting more "hits" in the system. You need to use a keyword only once for the computer to recognize it.

If using acronyms, use the written-out version as well as the acronym itself. For example, you would want to write out Bachelor of Science as well as using B.S. Because you do not know how the program searches for keywords, listing both forms will ensure that the program has every opportunity to locate your pertinent information.

Many books exist on the topic of keywords. Wendy Enelow's book, *Best KeyWords for Résumés, Cover Letters, and Interviews* (Impact Publications, 2003), provides a wide range of samples of how keywords can be incorporated into text. Use your industry's literature and professional organizations to get a feel for keywords specific to your field. Job listings are another good source for finding keywords; look for nouns and adjectives. Also review your skills list.

Remember to be truthful. Even though you want to garner as many hits as possible, you do not want to add a bunch of keywords to your résumé that are not appropriate for your situation, even if those words are on every keyword list you review for your industry.

E-mailed Résumés

Unless specifically stated otherwise, always paste your résumé into the body of an e-mail when using this option for sending. Many companies will not open attachments for fear of viruses and worms but also because they may not be able to open the attachment depending on the software used to create it.

To paste your résumé, convert it into an ASCII document to ensure that the recipient can read it. Not everyone is equipped to read HTML coding, and your "fancy" hard copy version may include HTML.

ASCII (pronounced "askee") stands for American Standard Code for Information Interchange and can be read by most systems. To save your hard-copy version as an ASCII version, open the document in your word program and "Save as" a plain-text file using a new file name. Other programs may allow you to save as an ASCII (DOS) file. At this point get rid of all the stuff that makes your résumé look pretty.

Highlight all of the text and change it to Courier size 12. Change your heading information so that it is listed in a logical order. Left-justify the document, get rid of any tables, and remove any tabbed spaces. Change any bolded, italicized, or underlined characters to normal text.

If you have added a picture graphic in the form of a line, delete it. You can add a line using a keyboard character. Generally speaking, any character that you create with the keyboard can be used in an ASCII document, but stick to the simpler ones to be safe. A line of separation can be created by using a series of dashes, asterisks, periods, or the tilde sign. For bulleted items, do not try to make any warp-around text line up with the sentence above it by using the space bar. In other words, let your text wrap around naturally, and use hard returns (the "Enter" key) to create space between sections or paragraphs (but not within paragraphs).

If your résumé is longer than one page, delete all the headers that state your name and page number on the subsequent pages. In the e-mail version, the recipient will not know if your original résumé was one page or more. However, the recipient will not be able to view the entire résumé in the e-mail screen. He or she will need to scroll down to read further. This means that, similar to your hard copy version, you should highlight your qualifications near the top of the résumé. Make your reader want to see more.

When you are done reformatting, close the document and reopen it. At this point you look for any odd-looking characters that may be left over. Change these as needed, save your changes, and you have an ASCII document. You may want to give your ASCII résumé a test drive by e-mailing it to yourself or a friend to see how it comes across in different programs.

Online Résumé Databases

Many online résumé databases allow you to post your résumé online. Often this includes walking through a process where you enter your information step-by-step. (Some now allow you to upload your résumé directly from its original file, such as a Word file.) When posting your résumé into these systems, use your ASCII résumé that has already been created and proofread. This will make the process much easier on you and will ensure that your information is already in an acceptable format.

When looking for jobs, many companies will provide a link to their own website or an e-mail address. Follow the instructions the company provides. If the ad asks you to e-mail your résumé, e-mail it—do not use the link to automatically send your résumé that you have uploaded. Cut and paste your ASCII résumé and address it to the e-mail address given. You want your résumé to go directly to the company as quickly as possible.

If the company provides a website, follow the link and look for another link with information about current openings. Some will provide a different e-mail address or contact information from what is listed on the job board site, or the company may use its own form for you to cut and paste your résumé. Use this option rather than using the quick link on the job board site. Again, you want your résumé to go directly into the company's database.

The following are some of the bigger job search sites:

America's Job bank: http://www.ajb.dni.us

CareerBuilder: http://www.careerbuilder.com

TrueCareers: http://www.careercity.com

CareerPath: http://www.careerpath.com

HotJobs.com: http://www.hotjobs.com

Monster.com: http://www.monster.com

NationJob Network: http://www.nationjob.com

You may also want to check into:

CollegeGrad.com: http://www.collegegrad.com/

College Central: http://www.collegecentral.com

CollegeRecruiter.com: http://www.collegerecruiter.com

Experience: http://www.experience.com

InternshipPrograms: http://internships.wetfeet.com

InternWeb.com: http://www.internweb.com

MonsterTRAK: http://campus.monster.com

SummerJobs.com: http://summerjobs.com

For a comprehensive overview of electronic résumés, refer to *Résumés in Cyberspace* (Barron's Educational Series, 2000) by Pat Criscito (or visit her website at http://www.patcriscito.com). In addition to an in-depth discussion on the subject, the author provides an extensive list of websites by industry and related subject matters.

Part IV

INTERVIEWING

Chapter 15

The Purpose of the Interview

Your cover letter asks for an interview. Your résumé shows why you should be invited for an interview. The purpose of the interview is to gain a job offer.

Notice that the purpose of the interview is not to get a job; it is to get an offer. This is an important distinction, particularly for new graduates. Why? Without a job offer, you have no decision to make. Also, if you go to every interview seeking an offer, you can hone your interview skills. In other words, take every interview offered you, regardless of whether you want the job. As someone new to the job market, the more practice you can get interviewing, the better off you will be.

Never turn down an interview, and always state that you are interested in the job, even if you are not. You can always politely decline later if you are offered the position. Besides, you may realize following an interview or two that you are in fact interested in the position; the additional information that you obtain during the interview could change your mind. If you turn down an interview, you will never know if the position is of interest.

While the interview is primarily for the interviewer to determine if you are a good match and if you are qualified, it is also a time for you to interview the company. Bear in mind that you are seeking a position that is well suited for you just as much as the interviewer is seeking someone qualified for the position. If you remember this, it can help with interview jitters.

Very few people actually like to interview. This includes the people conducting the interviews. Studies have shown that many people conducting interviews feel anxious and unqualified when doing so. It is also known that most people are not trained in conducting interviews. So in your job search you will run into all types of interviewers, from the inept to the skilled and trained professional interviewer. You need to be prepared for all types.

While there is no way to be prepared for every type of situation you may encounter, being prepared for the interview process is key. Interviewers are looking for someone who is qualified, communicates well, and will fit into the company culture. This is why your company research is vital. The more you know about the company the better.

Interviewers are also looking for someone who exudes professionalism. It is hard to define professionalism because it is a way of being that is learned over time. For someone with little "real world" experience, professionalism is, in all honesty, hard to come by. How do you combat this issue? It is like the age old dilemma of "How can I gain the experience needed to get a job if no one will hire me in the first place?" There are a number of steps you can take to help you on your way. If you follow the suggestions given here, you will be off to a good start. As you progress through your career, you will naturally develop your own professional style.

Know Thyself

First and foremost, you must have an understanding of who you are. Otherwise, you will not be able to communicate this in an interview, and the purpose of the interview is for the employer to determine who you are, what you can offer, and to get a glimpse of your personality. When you have a thorough understanding of yourself, you can then present yourself in the best possible light. You can show employers what you want them to see.

This is where your self assessments are key. Take advantage of the tools listed earlier in this book, seek the guidance of career counselors, and use the career resources available to you through your school (most colleges offer career services to alumni, so if you graduated without using these resources, it is not too late). Too many people do not take advantage of these resources; those that do will be well ahead in the game. Whether you are feeling very clear in your career path or have just graduated with a specialized degree and are trying to determine a career path, getting a good grasp of who you are will help you immensely in the interview process. Because you will be required to answer difficult questions not only about your skills but also about your behavior, you need to know what you would do in a hypothetical situation and how to best present your answer.

Just as important, having a good grasp on who you are will help you determine if you like what you learn about a company and its culture; you are conducting an interview yourself, so you need to know what it is you want and what type of atmosphere is best suited for your personality. Just as you would not buy an expensive suit without first trying it on, nor do you want to "buy" a job that way, either.

Career coaches Sande Foster and Susan Tovey of Catapult Your Career (http://www.catapultyourcareer.com) stress the importance of using assessment tools in your career search. Assessments help you determine where you are best suited and what type of position is best for you. They give the example that not everyone is a leader, and that is okay. Yet so many people walk into an interview and, when asked where they want to be in five years, answer "management" because they think that this is what the interviewers want to here. Similarly, some people seek positions that are not well suited to them but pursue that path due to parental or societal pressures or for monetary reasons, not realizing that money may not be one of their true motivating factors.

As discussed, assessments can also help you determine your attitude toward work and your skills. You need to be able to clearly articulate your skills and personal attributes. Without fully exploring these issues, you may come up short when answering questions during the interview. Knowing your behavioral traits will also help you in the interviewing process. You will be asked hypothetical questions, such as, "What would you do in this situation?" followed by a specific problem you may encounter on the job. Many grads have limited work experience to show what they have done in the past. You need to have a strong sense of self to know how you would most likely react in the given situation and why; and be able to show why that response is appropriate.

This self-awareness is also important because just having a degree is not enough anymore. You need to be able to demonstrate qualities that show you will be a good employee despite of, or in addition to, your education. This is not necessarily an easy task, but it is worth the time and effort. However, as Foster and Tovey point out, you need to be *ready* to do this kind of self-assessment. If you are not at a point where you are willing to put in the time and effort, you can "go through the motions" but it will not mean as much. If you are serious about finding a career and succeeding in the interview process, you must be willing to take a good look at yourself.

The bonus to learning more about yourself is that you are the only person who can toot your own horn in the interview. No one else is going to go in there and do it for you. When you know what your best skills are, your most desirable attributes, and your personality traits that will help you succeed in your chosen career, you can then go in and speak to those things in the interview. Those who do not do this self-research will not have as good an idea of what to highlight during the interview, so you will be ahead of your competition. Reviewing your strong points is also a huge confidence booster that will help you tremendously in the interview. If you are

able to exude confidence and show conviction in your answers because you know these things to be true about yourself, you will be much more successful.

Foster and Tovey also discuss the benefits of internships in developing professionalism. This type of real-world experience is invaluable; students are able to learn firsthand the dynamics of company culture and begin developing their own sense of professional style. These experiences will put them ahead of the competition. If you are still in school and are able to obtain an internship position, take full advantage of the opportunity.

Know Thy Company

Once again, company research is vital when you are going into an interview. You will be asked, "Why do you want to work here?" and "What do you know about the company?" You need to be able to answer these questions, so do your research.

Most companies have websites these days. This is an excellent place to start. Your interviewers will be impressed when you are able to discuss how your personal values are closely related to the company's mission statement, which you will be able to summarize. Read the entire website. Get a feel for how the company operates. If the company is public, look up its stock information. Then cover the basics. What does the company do? How big is it? Is it national or international? How many employees does it have? How often does it hire? Does it promote from within? Who are the major competitors? How does this company's philosophy differ from those of its competitors? Also review any employee biographies that may be listed on the site. You never know; one of those people might be interviewing you. If you have an idea what the personnel are like, you have a better chance of striking a chord with them.

If possible, you may want to visit the company as well, depending on the type of business and what, if any, security measures they have in place. At the very least, you may be able to see what the employees look like; this will give you a good idea of how to dress for the interview, as well as give you clues to the company culture. A company where employees show up in suits is much different from a company where employees show up in jeans.

If you were referred by someone in the company, ask as many questions as you can if the person is willing. The more inside information you can obtain, the better. Go in prepared.

Prepare, Prepare, Prepare

Preparation also includes learning as much as you can about interviewing. "We are not taught how to interview," says Kevin Cox of Career Unfolded (http://www.careerunfolded.com). The irony is that an interview is such an integral part of our career success, yet many people do not know how to interview well. "Graduates learn discipline through school, but they do not learn what employers want," says Cox. Because of this, he recommends students take advantage of the career services available through the school (are you noticing a trend here?). The career counselors can help students learn what employers are looking for and learn how to show that they can meet those needs.

Because gaining a full understanding of what employers look for comes from time and experience in the "real world," Cox recommends taking advantage of the information interview as well. Talk to people who work in your desired field. Ask as many questions as possible. He warns against assuming that your success will follow the same path as the other person's success. This is not always true; each person is unique, but knowing how another person reached success can certainly be helpful.

Going into the interview prepared also includes having an idea of what you will be facing and being prepared with your answers. Employers have a need; you need to demonstrate that you can meet that need. If you go into the interview feeling desperate, it will show, says Cox. Having an idea of what to expect will boost your confidence.

Michael S. Levy of Career Designers Services, LLC (http://www.careerdesigners.com), compares the interviewing process to preparing for a marathon. Runners begin preparations up to a year in advance. While this may not always be practical for the job seeker, the sooner you can begin preparing the better. Levy says of the interview, "It's much more than a day of answering questions and hoping to get a few right. It's much more than putting on your best attire and flashing a lot of smiles. It's much more than dazzling the interviewer with your technical expertise. It's a day to give it 'all' you've got."

Practice, Practice, Practice

An actor would not go out onstage without first practicing the role; similarly, you should not go into the interview without first practicing. Using the marathon metaphor, just as runners need to constantly work their bodies, so too should you do practice runs before the real thing.

Kevin Cox stresses the importance of practicing for the interview. He advises all of his clients to videotape a practice interview and then watch it for things to change. And he does not recommend just doing this once; he recommends four to five times. For the college student, the career resource center is an excellent setting in which to practice interviewing. Many centers are set up to video and comment on practice interviews. As mentioned elsewhere, many of these career services are open for use by alumni as well, so there is really no excuse for not taking advantage. For other resources, seek a qualified career counselor or career coach.

Practice and preparation go hand in hand. You want to be prepared to answer tough questions and practice answering them with confidence and control. Preparation includes knowing what you will say in response to those questions. Practice is finding your natural voice and rehearsing posture and communication techniques when responding. This is why your self-assessments and review of your past is so important.

When reviewing your strengths, review all areas of your past that demonstrate skills and attributes that can be helpful on the job. Look to your educational background, volunteer activities, sports activities, clubs and memberships, employment, and any other situations where you used your talents. (Be wary of using political or religious affiliations, however, as you want to avoid all references to these subjects when interviewing). Make a list of everything you can come up with, and compare it to a list of questions you may encounter in an interview. (There are many resources available that list all kinds of possible interview questions.) What from your past demonstrates how you can solve problems? What shows your ability to make decisions? How have you been able to demonstrate communication skills? When have you needed to use your technical skills?

After you have mined your past, put all this information together with what you know of yourself from your assessments. Carefully review everything you now have in front of you. This is what you will draw upon to answer questions. As you are faced with those tough questions, you will have a list you can readily draw from to compose your answers. However, you will not be able to take this list to an interview with you (although you may be able to take in a "cheat sheet," discussed later) so you need to practice the skills necessary to be able to pull this information from your brain when necessary.

Although you do not want to memorize word-for-word how you will answer certain questions (because you do not want to sound rehearsed), you will want to memorize the overall message you mean to convey. We all have moments where something slips our mind or we are not able to pull out the information we want at just the right moment. Under stress, it can be even more difficult to remember everything you need to know at the precise moment. When you are facing five senior members of a corporation who just asked you to provide a specific example of a time when you solved a problem, you might cave under pressure. This is why practice is so important. If you have had a chance to go through the motions, even if the rehearsal is not stressful, you will have experience to draw upon when facing the real thing. These practice sessions allow you to review not only the answers you provide but the tone and energy in your voice, how you carry yourself, and any unconscious movements you may have a tendency to make. The more interviews you are involved in, the better you will become at interviewing. Why not give yourself a head start and practice rather than using your first real interviews as your practice sessions?

Chapter 16

Communication Techniques

The phrase "Actions speak louder than words" is true. Most communication takes place non-verbally. In addition to preparing your answers, you want to prepare how you will act before, during, and after the interview. Another common phrase, "It's not what you say but how you say it," also holds a lot of truth. This chapter will review some communication tips that will help you present your best self.

You will likely first speak to the interviewer over the phone to schedule the interview. As obvious as it might seem, be sure to have a professional message on your answering machine or voice mail. If you want someone to leave a message regarding possible employment, do not use a flippant message, blaring music, or anything else that could be off-putting. State your name clearly or record your phone number so the caller will know that the correct number was dialed. When speaking to the person scheduling the interview, whether it is the owner of a small company or a member of the human resources department of a large conglomerate, be polite and professional. (Remember, many people will ask human resources or administrative person-

nel what their impressions of you are.) If possible, eliminate background noise. Speak clearly and directly into the receiver. Stand up while you are talking so you can breathe easier. Sometimes even this short conversation can get your adrenaline rushing—and why not? All the hard work you put into your résumé and cover letter has paid off!

Once the interview has been scheduled, be sure you are clear about any directions given you and where the interview will be held. Most interviews will take place onsite at the company, although some may be conducted elsewhere. If needed, make a dry run ahead of time to see how long it will take you to get there and to ensure that you know where you are going.

On Your Way

On the day of the interview, leave a little earlier than planned to ensure you arrive on time. You never know if traffic will be particularly bad or if you will face some other delay. Take the phone number of the company with you just in case you do get held up somewhere. Once you arrive, you can take a minute or two in the car or restroom to take a few deep breaths, touch up your hair or makeup, and give yourself a few moments to mentally prepare. Review any notes. Run through your qualifications. Give yourself a pep talk.

Take advantage of deep breathing on your way to the interview and throughout. Breathe in through your nose, hold the breath for a second or two, and breathe out your mouth. Granted, you do not want to do this in the interview, but a few deep breaths beforehand can help you relax. During the interview, remind yourself to breath as deeply and evenly as possible. When you need a moment to pause and reflect on a question, this is a good time to take a breath as well. And when the other person is talking, take the opportunity to breathe deeply—but do not get so focused on your breathing that you forget to listen closely. Practice breathing during your mock interviews.

Putting Your Best Face Forward

Upon arrival, introduce yourself to the person at the desk or your first point of contact. Use your first and last name and state that you have an appointment with so-and-so. Be polite, shake hands if appropriate, and be sure to smile!

Smiling is a universal sign of friendliness. Do your best to smile naturally. If you are overly nervous, this can be difficult and it may feel (and possibly look) forced. As silly as it sounds, imagine you are talking to your best friend or someone you really admire; whatever it takes to help your face relax. When you meet the person (or persons) you will be interviewing with, give another smile and shake hands if initiated by the interviewer.

Smile as appropriate off and on through the interview. Some people get very nervous and sit through the interview with a goofy grin stuck on their faces the whole time. Again, practice can help in this area. There will likely be a mix of lighthearted moments with serious ones throughout the interview. Obviously, you want to use appropriate facial expressions throughout. Smiling at an inappropriate time will be a tip-off to your nervousness at best or make you seem completely out of touch and insincere at worst. Practice, practice, practice. Review your video sessions for what your face is saying about you that your words are not.

Walk the Part

You will be watched as you enter the room and walk to the interviewing location. Be sure to stand tall, hold your head up, and look forward. You want to exude a confident walk but not an arrogant one. If you hold your shoulders too far back and your chest too far forward, you may give the wrong impression of being cocky. On the other hand, if your shoulders are hunched forward and you look down, you will come across as submissive and insecure. Aim for a friendly, easy gait, but one that is not overly relaxed. Wear shoes that are comfortable and that you can walk in easily. Watch for slippery soles or too-high heels. The last thing you need to be thinking about is if you will slip and fall.

A Rule of Thumb

The handshake has been given a lot of attention for such a quick gesture. However, it is widely used in the business world, so you might as well get a grip on proper technique. When you extend your hand, do so with the palm facing sideways. If your palm is either facing up or down, it can give the wrong signal, such as over-aggressiveness or passivity. And while you have undoubtedly been told to give a firm handshake, watch that you do not attempt to crush the other person's fingers. You may inadvertently grip too hard or too loose if you are nervous. A good rule of thumb is to match the firmness of the other person, particularly when shaking the hand of someone in authority or higher up on the career ladder. How long should you shake? About three "pumps" is sufficient.

To Sit or Not to Sit?

Do not sit down until you are motioned or asked to do so. If the interviewer forgets to invite you to sit, politely ask where he or she prefers you to sit during the interview. If you are interviewing at the person's desk, do not place any of your personal items on the desk, as this could be seen as a violation of personal space.

Once you are in your chair, be observant of how you position yourself. If you lean back in your chair, for example, you may be perceived as laid back or lazy. Leaning back with your hands behind your head could be interpreted as being cocky. Sit up straight, leaning slightly forward. This will demonstrate that you are alert and interested in what the interviewer has to say.

As for your legs, uncrossed is best, although crossing at the ankles or knees could be okay. Do not cross one foot over the other knee, as this is too casual a posture for an interview.

If you are at the person's desk or at a conference table, do not prop your arms up on the desk or table. If at the desk, use your lap to take notes on the pad of paper you will have brought with you for taking notes (see more on this in chapter eighteen). If you are at a table, you may use it instead of your lap, as the table is common ground for everyone involved.

All in a Name

When you meet people in the interview process, whether you are introducing yourself to the receptionist when you walk in or are meeting the CEO, always introduce yourself by first and last name. Address the other person as Mr. or Ms. so-and-so. Do not address the other person by first name unless you are invited to do so. This shows respect of the other person, and it demonstrates professionalism. Remember, you are meeting a future boss, not a new best friend.

A Common Thread

People hire others like themselves. Kevin Cox of Career Unfolded recommends building rapport with those doing the interviewing. There will likely be a little bit of small talk at the start of the interview. If you are able, try to find something you have in common with the interviewer. You may see a calendar on the wall of famous golf courses; if you are an avid golfer, you can casually ask if the interviewer is as well. Take tips from the décor and the direction of the conversation. If you are not able to develop a rapport toward the beginning, work on developing it throughout the interview. When you are able to hit upon something you have in common, both of you will likely feel a little more relaxed. This will also add a pleasant and familiar feel to the interview, which communicates to the interviewer that you are friend, not foe. And it will help the interviewer remember you.

One useful tool for building rapport is to use the mirroring technique. This is similar to the game you may have played as a child where you copied a friend's movements. In this technique you do in fact mimic the other person's movements, gestures, and manner of speaking but not to an obvious degree. For example, if the interviewer rests her arms on the chair's armrests, you follow suit and do the same. If he crosses his legs, you cross your legs a moment or two later. You can also mirror the tone and pace of the other person's voice. If you are interviewing with a soft speaker, lower the volume of your voice rather than talking loudly. Conversely, if the other person is a loud speaker, you can raise your voice slightly but not to the point where you are the louder talker. Mirroring can be very effective if used properly and in moderation. "I believe it's a very effective way of building rapport," says Cox. "It gives the subtle impression that you're likeable." Because this technique can be obvious if not done well, or distracting if you are concentrating too much on what the interviewer is doing rather than saying, it is a good one to practice in your video sessions.

Eye to Eye

I know one business owner who briefly met a job candidate as she was being given a tour of the facilities during the interview. After she had left, he contacted the hiring committee and told them that she was absolutely not to be considered for the position.

The hiring committee was stunned. The candidate had given a good interview. She had all the right qualifications. She had answered the questions well. She seemed to have the motivation to do the job well.

What had made the owner come to such a rapid and surprising conclusion?

She had failed to look him in the eye when she was introduced.

In less than 10 seconds, this candidate lost the job.

It is considered polite in our society to look others in the eye when they are speaking. Again,

nerves can make this simple recognition an awkward element in an interview. You do not want to stare down your interviewer, nor do you want to be constantly looking away. To avoid feeling like you are staring, focus on the other person's forehead and the space between the eyes. This will give the impression of looking at the other person without staring. As it feels natural, look away when in thought or answering a question, but take care not to look down. This can make you look weak. Instead, look off to the side or up as you are formulating your thoughts. Be sure to look at the interviewer again as you begin to speak or when another question is asked. Also be wary of having "shifty" eyes during the interview. Nerves may cause you to look back and forth between the other person's eyes, which can be distracting to the person watching you. Also be careful of not looking away too much. Again, it all comes down to practice, particularly for those who are shy or do not consider themselves naturally social.

And be sure, especially when being introduced to your interviewer or other members of the organization, to stand (if you have been sitting and someone enters the room and you are introduced), give a firm handshake, and look the person in the eye while smiling in a friendly, open manner.

Your Voice

When talking about a prospective position, are you energized or do you speak in monotone? If you cannot convey any excitement about the position, the interviewer will not be excited about hiring you. You cannot convey excitement about a position without having some interest in it. Your voice will likely sound fake if you try to force enthusiasm for something in which you have little interest. It all comes back to knowing what career path is best for you, what you are best at, and why you are the best person for your chosen profession. If you know you are on the right path but are still having problems, consult your video tapes to see what you might change. It may be useful to spend some time with a vocal or acting coach to learn how to control your breathing and your voice.

Act the Part

There is a saying used in Alcoholics Anonymous that goes, "Fake it 'til you Make it." In other words, even if you feel that things are not going well or that you have no clue what you are doing, put on a happy face and pretend that you do, and eventually, with enough time and practice, you will not be faking it anymore. You will have made it! The same goes for interviewing. You may feel when you walk into the interview that you have no clue what you are doing, that you do not have the skills, or a myriad of other doubts that may be running through your head. Take a deep breath, use the techniques discussed here, and pretend that you are in total control. This will exude confidence, and in return, just by "faking" it, you will begin to feel more confident as well. Studies show that if you force yourself to smile even when you do not feel like it, the simple, physical act actually causes a physio-

logical response that makes you begin to feel better. You can make yourself feel more confident by using these physical techniques. You will feel more confident and powerful because you will be using your whole body. You will breathe easier because you will sit or stand tall, and this in turn will help keep your mind fresh and clear for the extent of the interview.

Career Coaches and Interview Professionals

If you feel that you need assistance in learning how to interview, you may want to consider using a career coach or interview professional (see the earlier discussion on career coaches). You will likely want to choose one that is certified. There are certifications for both career coaches and employment interview professionals. See Appendix II for more information.

Teena Rose of Résumé to Referral (http://www.resume bycprw.com) advises, "Anytime someone has one chance to make a great impression, they are smart to be coached or trained. . . . Once things are said or done, they can't be taken back. If making the right impression on a prospective employer is top on your list, then take your interviewing and speaking skills to the next level. Know what to expect in the interview, and don't fool yourself into believing you can wing it."

Chapter 17

The Big Day

Yes, you need to look good for your interview. Yes, you need to arrive on time. Yes, you need to take a few things with you. Have everything ready the day before so you will not feel rushed and do not forget anything. Some people recommend always having an "interview suit" pressed and ready to go in the event that you get called in for an interview on short notice—some people will call and ask if you can come in the same day. It is not a bad idea to be this prepared when you are seeking employment.

What to Wear

Our first impression of a person is made in less than a minute, often before a person even opens his or her mouth to speak. Yes, it is true: We are a visual society and how you look coming into the interview can definitely affect the outcome, no matter how well prepared you are or how well you answer the tough questions.

When you take the initiative to look good for the interview, you demonstrate that you are going to be a positive representative of the company. You are someone who pays attention to detail. And you are someone who respects the interview process and the interviewers.

You may have heard to dress for "one step above the position." This is still good advice. Some recommend that you always wear a suit to an interview. This is good advice in general. There will be times when you need to use your best judgment. Your geographical location and the local business climate will also influence how you dress for the interview; however, it is always better to be overdressed than underdressed. You really cannot make a fool of yourself overdressing unless you show up in formal attire.

In general, the following tips will help you determine what to wear to almost any interview. If in doubt, always err on the conservative side. Once you are employed, you will gain a feel for the company culture; until that time, do not risk appearing too casual, as this can hurt your chances of obtaining the job offer. Those in more creative fields may have a little more leeway, but again, a polished, professional look will work well in almost every situation. Those seeking employment in creative industries may need to put a little more thought or creative energy into their interview attire; for these people, it is essential to be "up" on current fashion trends. For most of us, however, sticking with the basics will work just fine.

For Men

Have at least one business suit available for interviewing (no one will remember if you wear the same one to a second interview). Pick one that is dark but not black. Navy, brown, or gray is best. Pinstripes may be okay if they are subtle. Wear a white or light-colored long-sleeve shirt underneath. Choose a tie that compliments the suit and is not too wide or too thin. It should hang down to just above the belt. In some instances, dress pants with a long-sleeve shirt, tie, and sport coat may be acceptable, but again, you must know the company culture to determine if this is appropriate. It should go without saying that your clothes should be clean and wrinkle free.

Shoes should be leather and compliment the suit. Brown shoes should be worn with a brown suit. Black shoes should be worn with gray or navy. Stick with solids; two-tone shoes can make a fashion statement, but you may not make the one you are aiming for.

If you have long hair, you may want to consider cutting it during your job search. You can then determine after you are hired if long hair is appropriate for your business. Even though long hair on men is more acceptable socially these days, it may not be appropriate for some businesses. The age of your interviewer may also be a factor. If you do keep your hair long, wear it in a style that is manageable or pull it back in a neat, clean ponytail. For short hair, choose a cut that is fairly mainstream, or try to style it that way for the interview. While you do not want to look completely unlike yourself, you do not want to create a first impression that can put you out of the running. Also keep hair color to a minimum. Men are taking advantage of highlights and color more often these days, but again, if it is not done conservatively, your hair color may have a negative effect. Keep highlights subtle and remember that this is not the time to opt for purple or blue hair dye, no matter how much you want to express your individuality.

Facial hair should be neatly trimmed or shaved. A clean-cut look is preferred nowadays for business. If you keep a beard, keep it short and combed. Do a check in the mirror before the interview to make sure it is free of crumbs. If necessary, be mindful of nose and ear hair; keep it trimmed if this is an issue for you.

Jewelry should be kept to a minimum. Men should wear a nice watch to the interview and perhaps a wedding band, but that is about it. Avoid gaudy rings, bracelets, and necklaces. Remove all earrings and any facial piercings such as eyebrow, nose, and tongue. These are not appropriate for an interview (and may not be appropriate on the job) and can be distracting if the interviewer is more focused on your hardware than on what you are saying.

If you have tattoos anywhere on your upper body, avoid the white shirt and instead go for a light color that will prevent anyone from being able to see the tattoos should you remove your suit coat for any reason. Also keep your sleeves down if you have tattoos on your forearms.

Because you will be shaking many hands and using your hands a lot during the interview, consider getting a manicure. At the very least, keep your nails short and clean. You do not want overly soft hands, but you may want to consider pumicing any rough calluses and using lotion.

Avoid using scented deodorant or heavy cologne. Some people are put off by strong scents; others are allergic. The same goes for hair products. It is best to go without cologne and use as few scented items as possible in your grooming.

Take a briefcase (soft or hard) that is in good condition and compliments your attire. You will be bringing additional résumés with you, copies of your references (in case you are asked—do not volunteer to provide this information), and a notebook and pens to take notes while you are there.

When you are prepped and fully dressed, stand in front of a full-length mirror and check yourself out! You look great and are ready to go.

For Women

Business suits are the best choice for women as well as men, and dark colors should be chosen. Women have more flexibility when it comes to adding color, although blouses should not be too bright or consist of busy patterns that can be distracting. Stick to solid colors. Ideally, your blouse will be long-sleeved or at least 3/4 length. Avoid sleeveless tops because you never know if you may remove your jacket for some reason. If you have tattoos on your arms or back, wear long sleeves and a darker shirt that will not leave your tattoos visible.

Wearing a business suit that is a skirt or pants is up to you. Gauge the local business climate and do your company research. When in doubt, go with a skirt, particularly if you are interviewing with a larger company or if you are interviewing for a more conservative profession. Skirt length should not be too short; around knee level is a good choice. Wear nylons that compliment your suit, but avoid black. Also avoid nylons with any patterning, such as fish-net or seamed, and avoid any "cutesy" nylons with decorations such as flowers. Always take an extra pair with you since they are prone to run at the least opportune times. And if you are the "natural" type, shave your legs if you plan on wearing a skirt to an interview, even though you will be wearing nylons. It should also be a given that your clothes need to be clean and wrinkle free. Avoid fabrics such as linens that tend to wrinkle the moment you put them on.

Wear flats or pumps with a low heel. Solid colors are best and should compliment your outfit. Avoid sandals, open-toed shoes of any kind, and pumps with a high heel. None of these options will give the impression you wish to make.

Choose a hairstyle that is fairly subdued. Keep it clean and neat, and avoid overly smelly hair products. Also be conscious of your hair color. If you have highlights, try to keep them subtle. Also avoid any vibrant hair colors (such as overly red or purple), any color that does not occur naturally, and coloring that combines too many shades. (Those in fashion, beauty, or other creative professions can get away with a bit more.) Also avoid very large hairstyles or those more appropriate for an evening out.

Makeup should be simple and as natural-looking as possible. Avoid heavy makeup as well. Use a light foundation and powder, minimal eye makeup, and a subtle shade of lip color.

If you wear earrings, choose something small and inconspicuous. Avoid long, dangling earrings. For those who have piercings beyond one in each earlobe, remove them. Also remove any other facial piercings such as eyebrow, nose, or tongue. Other jewelry should be kept to a minimum as well. A nice watch and one ring per hand is okay. So also is a light necklace that compliments, but does not distract from, your overall dress.

Make sure your nails are clean and well manicured. Consider having a professional manicure. Do not go in with excessively long fingernails, and make sure you do not have any nail polish that is chipped. If you do use nail polish, choose a subtle shade during your job search. This is not the time to use fire engine red, or worse, lime green. Stick with muted colors that compliment your skin tone. Use lotion to keep your hands smooth.

Use unscented deodorant and avoid perfumes. Many people do not like perfume and some are allergic. You do not want your interviewer sneezing the whole time because you wanted to smell nice.

Take either a purse or a briefcase that will allow you to carry what you need but that is not big and cumbersome. Bring extra copies of your résumé, a list of references just in case (but only present these if you are asked—do not volunteer to provide this information) and a notepad and pen to take notes. Choose a purse or briefcase (the soft ones are nice for women) that compliments your attire.

When you are prepped and fully dressed, stand in front of a full-length mirror and check yourself out! You look great and are ready to go.

A Few Words about Self-Expression

We express ourselves by the clothes we wear, our hairstyles, and how we present ourselves in general. It is perfectly understandable to want to express who you are in an interview as well. But keep in mind that an attitude of "they can take me as I am or leave me" may result in your being "left" too often. For the interview, it is always best to err on the conservative side. You can always put your piercings back in or wear the funky shoes if you later determine that the company culture can handle it. Otherwise, these things may be best left for evenings and weekends.

"Business casual" means something different to nearly every person you talk to. Some companies have strict dress codes, while some have virtually none. It is up to you to determine what you are comfortable with and what you can live with on a daily basis as far as company culture and policies are concerned.

At the Interview

Everyone says to show up a bit early for the interview for a reason. Time your arrival so that you arrive a bit before the scheduled start time. This allows you time to deal with any unforeseen delays, and you can use those few minutes beforehand to gather your thoughts and review your notes of accomplishments, strengths, and questions for the interviewer.

Take along a few mints with you even if you do not need them. Having them on hand can boost your confidence. Just be sure to finish the mint before the interview so you will not have anything in your mouth when you walk in the door. Gum is absolutely out.

Teena Rose says, "Hiring managers need to see beyond your exterior and focus on your skill set along with your possibilities. If the person with the power to hire you can't get past your personal appearance, then you're taking a step back instead of forward."

Make sure you are moving forward.

Chapter 18

Coping with the Difficult Questions

Early in my career, I interviewed with a woman whom I knew outside of the professional arena. She told me I could come in to discuss working with her. Because we knew each other, I figured she had a good grasp on the fact that I was qualified to do the job. I naively thought that we would be talking about a start date, salary, and the like.

The first question she asked me was, "Why do you want this job?" Embarrassing as it is to admit, I did not have an answer. After stumbling around for a few minutes, I finally said, "I don't know." As you can imagine, I did not get the job. (I also avoided her for a while after that out of sheer embarrassment.)

"Why do you want to work here?" is one of the easy questions. Obviously, you need to be prepared to answer this, as well as much more difficult questions, when going into the interview. Here are tips on some types of interview situations you may encounter, as well as how to deal with those tough (and not-so-tough) questions.

Types of Interviews

This is a good place to remind you that most people you interview with have not been trained in the art of interviewing. Also remember that many of those conducting interviews find the process to be just as uncomfortable as you do. Another reminder is that while company representatives are trying to determine if you are a good fit for the position and the company, it is also a time for you to determine if you like the people and the company that you are interviewing with.

One-on-One Interview

Many of the interviews you will be involved with will be between you and one other person, at least initially. This can both work for you and possibly against you. On one hand, this is a nice situation because you are with only one other person, which can help alleviate nerves. The flip side is that if you do not hit it off with this person, you do not have other interviewers with whom to develop a rapport. But fear not; with some practice, you can learn to communicate with all types of people. This will help you not only in your interviewing but in your subsequent career as well. The fact of life is that we all have to work with all types of people. The mirroring technique is perfect for this situation. Try to build a rapport as early as possible with your interviewer, and it will help the remainder of the interview go smoothly.

For the most part, the one-on-one interview will be the least nerve-wracking and a great way to gain interviewing experience. Just because the interview is between you and one other person does not mean you can be more casual or put less effort into the process. It just means that chances are good that your nerves may not be as shaky. Keep in mind that there is a good chance a second or even third interview will take place if you interview well in the first round (another reason not to take a one-on-one interview less seriously). These subsequent interviews often involve additional people.

Board Room Interviews

Being interviewed by more than one member of the company is extremely common. In this situation, you will be interviewed by more than one person. How many more? It all depends on the company. Ideally, you will be able to sit around a conference table so that you will be able to clearly see everyone and to use the table to take notes.

When being interviewed by a group of people, try to shake each person's hand and get their names before you are invited to sit. If you get a chance, make a note of each person's name so you will have them available for your follow-up thank you letters. Obviously, you will not be able use the mirroring technique in this situation; however, because more people are involved, you may be able to build a rapport with one or more of the

interviewers. This does not mean that you need to focus solely on these people; you want to have eye contact with each person involved. You also want to address each person in the room as you speak. One person will probably be leading the interview; do not allow yourself to fall into the habit of only addressing that person.

The Unscheduled Interview

Say you walk into an office to make a cold call and drop off your résumé. The receptionist asks you to sit while she delivers your résumé to the boss. Moments later she returns, saying that the owners (all 10 of them) would like to take a few minutes to speak with you. Then you find yourself sitting around a table being questioned. Unrealistic? Not entirely. While this situation is not likely to happen often, it can, and has, happened.

As you are conducting your job search, you need to be "on call" at all times. Remember the networking blurbs you composed earlier? You will want to review these and have your sales pitch ready to go on a moment's notice. A networking contact may introduce you to someone in the company in the middle of an informational interview. An interested employer may call you out of the blue and start asking you questions right then and there before scheduling an in-person interview. Your practice sessions will, once again, come in very handy in these surprise moments. So will the time and effort you put into being prepared. Know your strengths and be able to talk about them anytime, anywhere.

Phone Interviews

Sometimes an interview must take place over the phone for whatever reason. Remember that most of our communication takes place nonverbally? This obviously presents a problem when interviewing over the phone. You cannot see the other person's reaction, so you have to try and determine from the conversation how you are coming across. Acting your most professional is an absolute must with the telephone interview. You also need to pay much more attention to your voice and try to make the best word choices possible. Are you speaking with energy? Are you talking directly into the receiver? Do you have access to your notes about the company? And just as important, are you able to clear the room from any background noise? Loud roommates or screaming children do not make the best impression when part of a phone interview.

Ideally, the interview will be scheduled so you can have your notes and list of questions in front of you. There will be times when an employer might catch you off guard, however, so keep notes, a notepad, and a list of questions for potential employers near the phone at all times.

Some coaches recommend that you stand while you talk so that you are able to take deeper breaths. Walking around may also help you think and it lets you do something with your nervous energy. Because you cannot talk with your hands in a phone interview, remember to use your most powerful examples of who you are and what you have done.

And never, ever, eat, drink, or chew gum when conducting a phone interview.

Group Interviews

This type of interview is different in that not only are you likely to be interviewed by more than one member of the company, but you are also being interviewed at the same time as your competition. A company may call a group of

you in a separate room or interview all of you at once. You will likely be asked to introduce yourself to the whole group and give a brief summary of who you are. You will also have to answer interview questions in front of everyone else. For those who are shy or do not like public speaking, this interview may be extremely uncomfortable. This is what employers are looking for. This type of interview will likely be used for positions that require working with the public, making presentations, or interacting frequently with others. You may not know ahead of time if you will be facing this type of interview. If you walk into this situation, try not to let it take you off guard. Remember that everyone else there is in the same boat as you and they are likely feeling nervous about it, too.

What is the benefit for you in this type of interview? It is the one situation where you get to size up your competition! In almost all other interview situations, you have no idea who you are up against. But when you are interviewing at the same time as everyone else, you can observe what others do and make an effort to present yourself better. Keep in mind, however, that employers will also be watching you to see how you interact with the other candidates. You still want to be friendly and treat everyone with respect. If you act superior, ignore others, or are blatantly rude, you will eliminate your chances of being called back for a second interview.

Job Fairs

Take advantage of job fairs offered through your school. Some situations will require that you register through the career services office. Others will occur on a "walk in" basis. When you register through career services, you will likely have scheduled interviews with visiting companies. The open fairs allow you to peruse the booths and speak to recruiters as you are able. Either way, you need to show up prepared.

Patty Broadbent of Everything Careers (http://www.everythingcareers.com) is a former college recruiter for a large accounting firm. She notes that many students do not take advantage of the career fairs offered at their schools. Large companies that come to these fairs are actively recruiting and have developed a working relationship with the school. Why would you not take advantage of this opportunity?

When "working" the booths, Broadbent recommends that students visit every employer and be open minded about the process. Be prepared with a 20–30 second "blurb" to introduce yourself, state your major, what year you are in school, and what you are looking for. She then recommends that students take the initiative and ask recruiters to tell them about opportunities at the company rather than simply waiting for the recruiter to respond. Have copies of your résumé available to distribute because recruiters do look at them. This is a guaranteed opportunity to have your résumé read by a company that is hiring.

Broadbent reminds students to come to the job fair prepared just as they would be for any other interview. This means dressing appropriately, having an agenda, and being prepared to answer questions. The behavioral-based interview is common practice at job fairs just as it is anywhere else; students need to be able to provide concrete examples of their accomplishments. "Their past predicts their future success," she says. A recruiter may ask a question such as, "Tell me about a time when you've been effective in a team environment." Participants need to be ready to answer. Broadbent recommends that students look to their experiences for those qualities that are transferable and demonstrate teamwork, a positive attitude, and a strong work ethic.

The Questions

Many questions will be straightforward (How long did it take you to complete your degree?) Others will be vague (Tell me about yourself.) Some may seem completely irrelevant (What is your favorite color and why?) Some will test your skills, and others will seem like they came out of left field. Many resources exist on types of interview questions and how to answer them; such an in-depth discussion is beyond the scope of this book. It would be to your advantage to go to the library and borrow some books dealing strictly with interview questions and tips on how to answer them. This section will address some types of interview questions you might face and the areas that employers will likely ask about given that you are a new graduate and/or new to the workforce.

Aside from the relatively straightforward line of questioning, there are some interview styles you need to be aware of. The first, and perhaps most common, is the behavioral interview. In this type of interview, the basic premise is that the past predicts the future; more specifically, past behavior predicts future behavior. In other words, if you acted as a superior leader on a project for another company and can demonstrate that you did so, the theory is that you will be a superior project leader for the interviewing company as well.

Where does this leave someone with little or no work experience? That is a good question. Even though the interviewer will know you are new to the workforce, chances are you will still be faced with this line of questioning. "Tell me about a time when you had to resolve a difficult problem on your own. Give me an example of how you have demonstrated the ability to work as a team member and what were your contributions." You will need to mine your past for examples of how you demonstrated desirable skills, attitudes, and behaviors in the past. This may come from volunteer activities, club activities, school activities and projects, summer employment, and any other situation where you demonstrated the required skills. You will then need to show what you did and what the result was. In other words, you will need to tell a story.

When answering this type of questioning, use the STAR or SAR format: This stands for *Situation* or *Task*, *Action* taken, and end *Result*. When telling your story, relate the situation you faced or the task requiring attention. Describe how you took action to address the situation or task, and describe the end result. Obviously, you want to choose an example that had a positive outcome. No need to inform an employer that you tried something and failed. We have all done this at one time or another, but the interview is not the time to talk about it. Choose your best examples instead.

Another line of questioning is specifically designed to cause you stress. These are, not surprisingly, called stress questions. They may require quick thinking, put you on the spot, or use any number of techniques designed to make you sweat. For example, a group of interviewers may ask a mathematician to describe how to solve a simple, well-known problem. After the candidate gives a correct answer, the interviewers tell the candidate that the answer is incorrect and then watch the reaction. Another example may be if the interviewer picks up a pen and tells the candidate to "sell" it in 60 seconds or less.

The purpose of stress questions is to determine how you handle pressure. The interviewers are not so concerned with the answers as they are the reaction. With this in mind, you can relax a little when faced with stress questions because you understand the motive behind them. (For an in-depth discussion on stress questions, refer to the *Knock 'em Dead* series by Martin Yate.)

Other "questions" are not really questions at all but a test of your skills. Candidates applying for technical positions may be asked to solve a series of problems. A librarian may be asked to list the corresponding decimal numbers for a variety of nonfiction subject areas. An office manager may be required to compose a sample letter to a customer. Whatever your field, be prepared to be tested on the knowledge you claim to have; and ensure that if you claim it, you own it.

Some tests you may be asked to complete have nothing to do with your skills but with your personality. This type of testing is becoming more widely used to determine if you will be a good fit with the company culture or if the employer is looking for a certain type of personality. An executive may look for an assistant that has a very different psychological profile to help her in the areas that she is weak. Whatever the reason, you may find yourself facing a bunch of small circles labeled A, B, C, D and a number two pencil.

If you are absolutely opposed to taking this type of test, you can refuse, but this may disqualify you from the running. Ask what the purpose is for the testing, who will see it, and if you will have access to the results. Answers to these questions may help you decide what your preference is. If you take the test, remember that many of the questions are designed to trick you; for example, the same type of question is asked numerous times with different wording. In the end, though, most companies are simply looking for a stable individual to join their team and to see if the psychological profile matches what the candidate says about him or herself.

It will be obvious to the employer that you are a new graduate or new to the workforce and that you are most likely seeking an entry-level position. In addition to any number of other questions you may face, some are likely to be directly related to where you are in your career, your educational background, and your interests. Be prepared to answer questions along the following lines:

How long did it take you to complete your degree? Why?

Did you work your way through college?

What did you like the most/least about your summer employment?

Have you ever had conflicts with a boss? Did you like your previous boss?

Are your grades indicative of your potential?

Why did you choose your major? Why did you choose this career path?

What attracts you to this company? Where do you see yourself in five years?

What did you learn from your volunteer experience?

What would your professors say about you?

Why should we hire you over someone else?

What can you contribute to this position immediately?

How long do you think it will take you to be comfortable in this position?

What other positions in the company are of interest to you?

How long do you think you will stay with the company?

Tell me about your technical expertise.

Do you plan to pursue further education?

Many of the questions are designed to trip you up or make you say more than you intended to. For example, the answer to "Where do you want to be in five years?" can have multiple effects. On the one hand, the interviewer wants

to know if you will leave for another company after this one has invested time and money in training you. On the other hand, he or she may also be fishing to see if you want his or her job down the road. The interviewer may also be looking to see if you provide a more interesting answer than "in management" or "in a leadership position."

You will need to have a good grasp of your history and concrete examples to provide when answering questions. To do this, you can use a few tools in the interview to help you out.

Freddie Cheek of Cheek & Cristantello Career Connections (http://www.cheekandcristantello.com) offers some very helpful suggestions when answering questions. One technique is "answer plus one." This technique allows you to answer the question asked but also introduce an additional skill or selling point that you want to be sure to mention during the interview. Say that you want to discuss your project leadership skills, but the question you are asked about is what kinds of relevant coursework you took during college. You could say, "I took *list classes,* AND as the project leader of a parking lot design team (*name project*) in Civil Engineering 401 (*name of class*) I was able to direct our team to develop the only project later used and developed by the city." This way you answer the question but also demonstrate that you have leadership skills, something you would not have mentioned had you answered by just listing courses.

Cheek also recommends a similar technique, "trait plus answer." This technique is used when discussing "soft skills," or personality traits that are easy to talk about but rarely quantified in an interview. This technique allows you to say, I'm *name soft skill* because I do *name action* demonstrating the trait. For example, you may include somewhere in an answer, "I'm trustworthy because I regularly work with large amounts of money unsupervised in my role as cashier." Cheek says, "Validate the skill by backing it up with actions, duties, and responsibilities that you provide."

The final recommendation from Cheek is to present ways in which you are a job filler. In other words, show that you meet the needs of the company. Ask the interviewers to describe the ideal candidate, and then speak to how you meet the requirements. Ask what the other candidates have been lacking, and show that you have those skills. Ask about the main projects that will be taking place immediately in the position, and then talk about how your experience is directly related to that kind of work. Employers want to know what you can do for them. Use these techniques not only to demonstrate what you can do, but also to help control the direction of the interview in your favor. (See also the résumé sample on page 133.)

Your Tools

Take extra copies of your résumé: one for each of your interviewers, if needed, and one for yourself. By having your résumé in front of you, will you have an instant reminder of your most impressive accomplishments, as well as a general reference when it comes to dates or other specifics you may draw a blank on when feeling under pressure. Many interviewers will also refer to your résumé as they proceed through the interview. When you have it right in front of you, you can follow along and not miss a step.

Perhaps the most important tool you will take with you is a notepad and pen. Use this to take notes throughout the interview, both for reference during the process and afterwards as you compose your follow-up correspondence. If

you get funny looks from your interviewer(s), simply say that you would like to take notes because the interview is important to you. How can anyone argue with that?

Kevin Cox recommends using the notepad in a few helpful ways. First, you can jot down reminders of the most important things you need to remember for the interview: your achievements, skills, and topics you want to cover when appropriate. You can also write down your list of questions for the employer for that inevitable question toward the end of the interview: What questions do you have for us?

But perhaps one of the most useful tools for the notepad is that you can use it as both your cheat sheet and point of focus when answering questions. When faced with a tough question, take a moment to pause, look at your notebook (and steal a glimpse of your notes), and then answer the question. This will help you in that you not only have a cheat sheet in front of you but something to do rather than look around nervously. You can take that moment to reflect (which is also a sign that you are taking time to think rather than simply blurting out an answer), take a breath, and proceed with your response.

Another good technique is to answer the question with another question. If you would like clarification, ask. If the question is really vague, such as "tell me about yourself," you can ask if the interviewer would like to know about your academic background, employment background, or both. By returning a question you can buy yourself a few moments to prepare your answer.

Your Questions

There are a number of canned questions that you may have heard you should ask of your interviewer. Frankly, these are good questions; but after these initial questions, seek to ask a few original ones as well. This is also the time to ask for clarification on any points that you would like more information. An example of a question that everyone asks is, "What are you looking for in a candidate?" or something along those lines. This is a great question if you are sincere; however, because everyone has been told to ask that question, it can come out sounding like something you read about in a book. Try to get creative when wording your questions or at least more direct. "Do you feel I meet your desired criteria for the position?" is one way to reword this question to your advantage. If the answer is yes, you are obviously a serious contender. If no, ask for clarification, and then explain why you do in fact meet the needs. If the interviewer says you lack technical skills, for example, show that you are a quick learner and give an example of a *situation* when you needed to learn something quickly,

how you went about doing so (*action*) and succeeded (*result*).

Because you did your company research before the interview, you can have a list of questions prepared that you would like to ask. Undoubtedly, some of those questions will be answered throughout the interview, but not all. Ask those that are still unanswered. Also take notes throughout the interview and make note of questions that arise. You can ask those questions as well.

One question you should never fail to ask comes at the close of the interview. This is when you ask, "What are the next steps?" or "When can I expect to hear from you?" Do not leave the interview open-ended. Find out what the timeframe is and what the next phase of the interviewing process will be. Restate your interest in the position and thank your interviewers for their time. Then go home and write your thank you letter or letters.

Chapter 19

After the Interview

What now? First and foremost, write your thank you letters to the interviewers. If needed, send a follow-up letter if you do not hear anything. In most cases, however, you will hear from the employer with one of three options. You did not get the job, you are invited in for a second (or third) interview, or you are offered the job.

We will start with the positive: You are offered the job. Congratulations! All of your hard work paid off! Now is the time to confirm the offer and write your letter of acceptance, outlining the offer as you understand it. If there are any discrepancies, you will be able to discuss them with your new employer. Now is also the time to write letters to anyone else you may have interviewed with to thank them for their time and consideration and inform them that you have accepted a position elsewhere.

What if you are offered the job and decide you do not want it? You need to politely decline. Whether or not you choose to give a reason is up to you, but be sure to give a positive reason, not that you did not like the people you interviewed with (even if this is the truth) or that you were not impressed with the company (even if this is the truth). Simply say that you do not feel this is

the best match for you or that now that you know more about the position, you realize you are looking for something more along the lines of such-and-such. Thank the interviewers for their time and offer and wish them all the best.

Do not be afraid to turn down an offer if you feel that the company or position is just not right for you. If you are still interested in the company, say so—there may be other opportunities that you are unaware of, and because the interviewers obviously like you, they may be able to offer something else or guide you to the appropriate department with a referral. However, if you have a gut feeling that it just is not right, follow that feeling. Even if you are somewhat desperate for a job, you are better off holding out for the right position than forcing yourself to work in a job or environment that is not for you. This will only lead you to extending your job search and perhaps experiencing a negative work experience or outcome in the meantime. Be respectful of yourself and the employer and do not put either one of you in this situation; besides, if the employer did not feel you were right for the position, he or she would not hesitate to say no to you.

If you have been called in for a second interview, be sure to review all of your notes and tips on interviewing. The fact that you have been called back in is a good sign—you obviously did well enough in the first or second interview to warrant another. Remember that you will likely be interviewing with additional people at the follow-up interviews and that you may be facing tougher questions. There may also be the chance that you will be tested on your skills if you have not been already.

In the first interview, you took notes and made more notes following the interview. Review these carefully, analyzing what went well and where you could have improved or where you wanted to emphasize a point that was not made. These are the issues you will want to weave into the conversation on the next go-around. You may also have additional questions now that you know more about the company and the position. Write these down so that you do not forget to ask.

This is also the time to review your assessments for those examples of what you have done well and how. You will need to be able to answer those behavioral-based questions, and the more stories you have to tell, the better. If possible, avoid repeating the answers you gave the first time if your original interviewer is present; but keep in mind that he or she will not remember everything you said, so if you are limited in your answers, stick with the best ones.

Finally, congratulate yourself on having made it this far. Think about it: Your résumé was culled from tens or hundreds of other applications. You then wowed them enough in your first interview to be called back for a second. This is no small feat! Out of the possible hundreds of applications, you are now one of the few. Take the boost of confidence that comes with knowing this and go in and give an even better interview than you did the first time.

And what if you do get that letter or phone call stating that another candidate was chosen? First, do not think of yourself as a failure. You made it all the way to the interview, which is more than most of the other applicants can claim. Congratulations! Second, remember that rejections will happen; not every job is right for every person. Everyone involved in this process is trying to find a good fit, including you. Ultimately, you want to find the position where both you and the employer believe you are the perfect person for the job.

When you do receive this letter or call, however, take advantage. Even though no one enjoys being turned down, make the most of the situation. First, thank your interviewers again for their time and consideration. Then politely ask where you were lacking in relation to the other candidate. This is not an easy question to ask, but it can give you valuable insight. If you need to practice asking this question, do, because it is a good one. While some may prefer not to answer, many people will, particularly if you are gracious and sincere. People like to help others, and your interviewers are no exception. Perhaps your technical skills were just not quite as strong, or perhaps they felt that the other person had a slightly better education. Now you have information you can work with for your next interview. How can you present your technical skills better? How can you show that your education meets the needs of potential employers? Use this information to craft better answers and examples to questions. Or maybe you will determine you need to brush up on your skills or enroll in some continuing education. Whatever the case, having the knowledge, however hard it is to ask for it, is much better than continuing to make the same mistakes.

Use every opportunity you can to learn more about yourself, and your career will thank you for it in the long run. This is your life we are talking about!

Contributors

Résumés At Work
Trish Allen, BA, CPRW, CEIP
PO Box 1416, Stafford 4053 Qld
Australia
+61 7 3357 3353
resumesatwork@optusnet.com.au
http://www.resumesatwork.com.au
Page 115

Best Résumés
Ann Baehr, CPRW
122 Sheridan Street
Brentwood, NY 11717
(631) 435-1879
resumesbest@earthlink.net
http://www.ebestresumes.com
Pages 67, 78, 86, 88, 199

Career Designs
Carla J. Barret, CCM
6855 Irving Rd.
Redding, CA 96001
(530) 241-8570
http://www.careerdesigns.com
Page 102, 180

A Personal Scribe, Résumé Writing & Design
Rosie Bixel, member NRWA

1913 NE 88th Ave.
Portland, OR 97220
(503) 254-8262
aps@bhhgroup.com
http://www.bhhgroup.com/resume.asp
Pages 71, 92

Cheek & Cristantello Career Connections
Freddie Cheek, CCM, CPRW, CWDP
4511 Harlem Road #3
Amherst, NY 14226
(716) 839-3635
fscheek@adelphia.net
http://www.cheekandcristantello.com
Page 133

Competitive Edge Résumés
Carolyn Cott of Competitive Edge Résumés
1372 Nathan Hale Drive
Phoenixville, PA 19460
(610) 917-0093
http://www.competitive-edge-resumes.com
Pages 62, 63, 64, 118

Dynamic Résumés of Long Island, Inc.
Donna M. Farrise
300 Motor Parkway
Hauppauge, NY 11731

(800) 528-6796 or (631) 951-4120
http://www.dynamicresumes.com
Pages 125, 188

Careers by Choice Inc.
MJ Feld, MS, CPRW
205 E. Main Street, Suite 2-4
Huntington, NY 11743
(631) 673-5432
mj@careersbychoice.com
http://www.careersbychoice.com
Pages 68, 79, 89, 135

Custom Résumé and Writing Service
John Femia, BS, CPRW
1690 Township Road
Altamont, NY 12009
(518) 872-1305
Customresume1@aol.com
http://www.customresumewriting.com
Pages 70, 77, 81 82, 106

Career Directions, LLC
Louise Garver, CPRW, CEIP, CMP, MCDP, JCTC
115 Elm Street, Suite 203
(860) 623-9476
Enfield, CT 06083
888-222-3731
TheCareerPro@aol.com
http://www.ResumeImpact.com
Pages 72, 84, 100, 112, 121, 146, 181

Guarneri Associates
Susan Guarneri, CPRW, NCCC, CEIP
1905 Fern Lane
Wausau, WI 54401
(866) 881-4055
resumagic@aol.com
http://www.resume-magic.com
Pages 73, 83, 148, 150

Right-On Résumés
Maurene Hinds, MFA, CPRW
rightonresumes@msn.com

http://www.maurenejhinds.com
Pages 98, 198

Arbridge Communications
Jan Holliday
Harleysville, PA 19438
(215) 513-7420
info@arbridge.com
http://www.arbridge.com
Pages 65, 74, 80, 184, 201

Top Margin Résumés Online
Gayle Howard, CCM, CPRW, CERW, CRW
PO Box 74
Chirnside Park Vic 3116 Melbourne
Victoria Australia
+61 3 9726 6694
getinterviews@topmargin.com
http://www.topmargin.com
Page 101, 104, 110, 127, 136, 138, 142, 192, 196

XSolutions Résumé Writing Service
Joseph Imperato, Pomona, New York
PO Box 76
Thiells, NY 10984
(845) 362-9675
resumes@xsresumes.com
http://www.xsresumes.com
Pages 75, 91

Dynamic Résumés
Diane Irwin
14 Aaron Court, Suite 2
Cherry Hill, NJ 08002
(856) 321-0092
dynamicresumes@comcast.net
http://www.dynamicresumesofnj.com
Pages 67, 129, 186, 190

Executive Essentials
Cynthia Kraft, CCMC
PO Box 336
Valrico, FL 33595

(813) 655-0658
cindy@career-management-coach.com
http://www.career-management-coach.com
Pages 87, 107, 142, 149

Résumé Suite
Bonnie Kurka, MS, CPRW, JCTC, FJST
(918) 494-4630 or (877) 570-2573
bonnie@resumesuite.com
http://www.resumesuite.com
Pages 108, 122, 187

A+ Résumés/A+ Business Services
Eva Mullen, CPRW
3000 Pearl Street, Suite 111
Boulder, CO 80301
(303) 444-3438
info@ABSonline.biz
http://www.ABSonline.biz
Page 94

Peripheral Pro
Melanie Noonan, CPS
West Paterson, NJ 07424
(973) 785-3011
peripro1@aol.com
Page 132

Write Away Résumé
Edie Rische, NCRW, JCTC
5908 73rd Street
Lubbock, TX 79424

(806) 798-0881
erische@door.net
http://www.writeawayresume.com
Pages 66, 76, 95, 99, 126, 131, 179, 185, 189, 191, 195, 200

Keraijen—Certified Résumé Writer
Jennifer Rushton, CRW
Level 14, 309 Kent Street, Sydney NSW 2000
Australia
+61 2 9994 8050
info@keraijen.com.au
http://www.keraijen.com.au
Pages 93, 123, 140, 152, 178, 182, 193, 194

ALPHA Résumé Writing & Career Services
Edward Turilli, MA, CPRW
918 Lafayette Road
North Kingstown, RI 02852
(401) 268-3020
edtur@cox.net
Pages 90, 119

Dream Catcher Résumés
Melissa M. Whitney, member PRWRA, NRWA, AORCP
19425 Soledad Cyn. Rd. Ste. B162
Canyon Country, CA 91351
(661) 713-7725
dcresume@socal.rr.com
http://www.dcresume.com
Page 114

Organizations

**Professional Association of Résumé Writers &
Career Coaches (PARW/CC)**
1388 Brightwaters Blvd., N.E.
St. Petersburg, FL 33704
(800) 822-7279 (toll-free) or (727) 821-2274
(727) 894-1277 (fax)
E-mail: PARWhq@aol.com
http://www.parw.com
Certifications:
Certified Professional Résumé Writer (CPRW)
Certified Professional Career Coach (CPCC)
Certified Employment Interview Professional
(CEIP)

**National Résumé Writers' Association
(NRWA)**
P.O. Box 184
Nesconset, NY 11767
(888) NRWA-444 (toll-free) or (631) 930-6287
E-mail: AdminManager@nrwaweb.com
http://www.nrwaweb.com
Certifications:
Nationally Certified Résumé Writer (NCRW)

**Professional Résumé Writing and Researchers
Association (PRWRA)**
(888) 86-PRWRA (867-7972, toll-free) or

(321) 752-0442
(321) 752-7513 (fax)
E-mail: info@prwra.com
http://www.prwra.com
Certifications:
Certified Résumé Writer (CRW)
Certified Expert Résumé Writer (CERW)
Certified Master Résumé Writer (CMRW)
Certified Electronic Career Coach (CECC)
Certified Career Research Professional (CCRP)
Certified Federal Résumé Writer (CFRW)
Certified Web Portfolio Practitioner (CWPP)

Career Masters Institute (CMI)
757 East Hampton Way
Fresno, CA 93704
(800) 513-7439
(559) 227-0670 (fax)
E-mail: swhitcomb@cminstitute.com
http://www.cminstitute.com
Certifications:
Credentialed Career Master (CCM)
Master Résumé Writer (MRW)

Index

Page numbers in **bold** indicate main discussion of a topic.